Do You Have What It Takes?

A Comprehensive Guide to Success After Foster Care
By Teens Who Have Been There

Edited by Kendra Hurley

Executive Editor
Keith Hefner

Editor
Kendra Hurley

Contributing Editors
Rachel Blustain
Al Desetta
Andrea Estepa
Sheila Feeney
Nora McCarthy

Cover and Design
Efrain Reyes
Jeff Faerber

Production
Efrain Reyes
Jeff Faerber

All drawn portraits by Martell Brown.
Art on p. 4 and p. 249 by Karolina Zaniesienko.
All other art by Youth Communication.

Cover photos are of current or past writers for *Represent: The Voice of Youth in Foster Care* and *New Youth Connections.*

At the time of this book's publication, all facts, figures, telephone numbers, organizations, Websites, etc., are accurate and active. If you find an error or change, please contact Youth Communication.

Printed in the United States of America   ISBN: 096612569X

Youth Communication is a registered trademark of Youth Communication/New York Center, Inc., a nonprofit youth development and publishing corporation.

Youth Communication®
224 W. 29th St., 2nd fl.
New York, NY 10001
212-279-0708
www.youthcomm.org

To the 25,000 young adults who age out
of foster care each year.

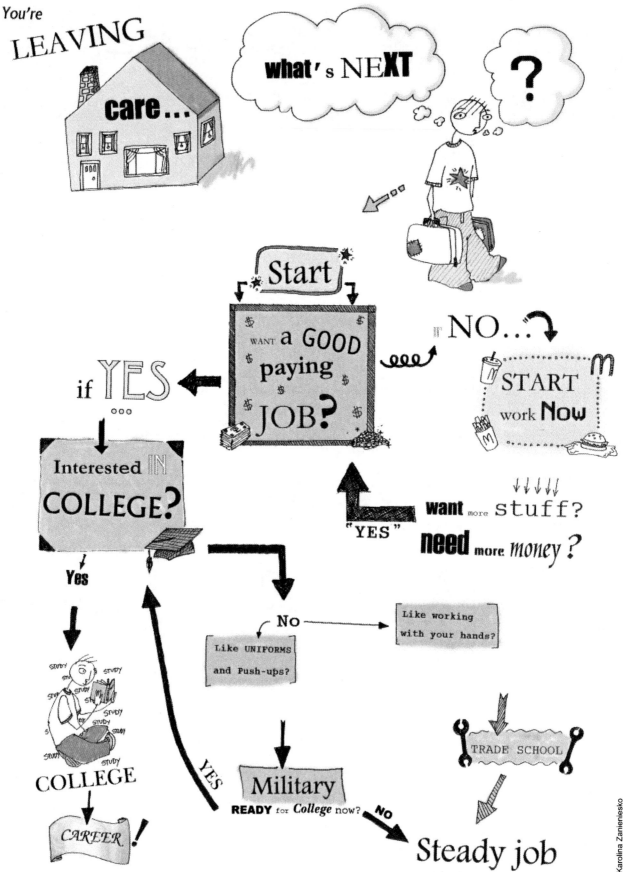

Table of Contents

$ Chapter 1: Manage That Money

Contents

Contents

Contents

Chapter 8: Options After Care

Chapter 9: Making a Plan

Contents

A Welcome for Independent Living Coordinators, Social Workers, Group Home Staff, Foster Parents... and Other Adults Who Care

In their eagerness to leave foster care, young people often underestimate how difficult it can be to live on their own. For more than 10 years, staff at *Represent*, the magazine written by and for teens in foster care, have watched young people charge off to their own apartments and then be surprised at how lonely they are. Or land their first job, and then quit due to conflicts with bosses. They are surprised to learn that being *emotionally* prepared is as important as having *practical* skills.

Anger, depression, loneliness, shame and other emotions make it difficult for teens to form healthy relationships. Practicing good hygiene, managing money and performing other chores depend on their ability to manage their emotions. But it's especially challenging to prepare young people for this side of life after care.

Why This Book Works

Do You Have What It Takes? helps young people understand and address these challenges.

The stories are written by veterans of the foster care system who have "been there," struggled, and learned. The hands-on activities will help prepare teens for the practical and emotional challenges they will face on the road to independence.

How to Use This Book

This book explores eight critical topics:

- Money management

- Jobs

- Getting an apartment

- Building a support system

- Navigating sex and relationships

- Hygiene and health

- Options after care

- Making a plan for leaving care that includes realistic goals

In each chapter, you will find personal stories, "how to" stories, and interviews with experts.

"How to" stories:

www.youthcomm.org

Advice From Experts on:

- Shopping smart, p. 44
- Managing work relations, p. 76
- Preparing for life's emotional challenges, p. 131
- Eating healthy, p. 160
- Applying to college, p. 274

Each chapter also includes an activity that you can use with groups of young people and worksheets young people can use on their own.

Activites:

Thought-provoking questions throughout the book will help you clarify your goals, values, and plans for leaving care.

Think About It:
pp. 30, 46, 75, 130, 240

Worksheets:

www.youthcomm.org

There is also a certificate at the end of the book on p. 307 to reward teens who successfully complete all worksheets.

Whether you work with groups or individual teens, all the stories provide rich material for discussion. Here are four ways you can use the stories and lessons.

1. Use the Stories With Teens in Groups

Teens (like the rest of us) often resist facing their issues. Using the stories in groups can help young people face difficult issues in a way that feels safe to them. That's because talking about the issues in the stories feels safer to teens than talking about those same issues in their own lives. The stories allow for some personal distance; they hit close to home, but not too close. As teens gain comfort talking about the issues in the stories, they usually become more comfortable talking about those issues in their own lives.

The activity pages in this book are designed to stimulate discussion around the stories and issues they address. They also provide hands-on activities for teaching independent living skills.

2. Use the Stories With Individual Teens

If a teen in your program or caseload is dealing with an issue raised in a story or chapter in this book, consider giving the teen a copy of this book and telling him or her that you thought the story might be of interest. You can give it to the teen in the spirit of "read it if you like," or you can tell the teen that you want to talk about the story. Teens say that reading the stories makes them feel less alone and more hopeful about meeting life's challenges. Adults often tell us that teens open up about their fears and concerns after reading a story. If you decide to talk with the teen about the story, the questions on pages 15 and 16 may be helpful. This book also has worksheet pages which a motivated teen can complete on her own.

3. Use the Stories With Individual Staff

Stories in this book can also be used to train staff, as well as foster parents, about the challenges facing youth preparing to leave care. Adults working with teens in foster care say that reading the stories gives them

www.youthcomm.org

new insights into what teens are thinking and feeling as they struggle their way towards independence, as well as new strategies for working with teens.

4. Use the Stories in Classes or Workshops With Adult Staff

The stories can be treated like case studies. Have staff or foster parents read and discuss them in the spirit of, "If I had this teen on my caseload, or in my classroom or program, or in my home, how would I feel? What would be challenging to me? What questions would I ask? What interventions would I use? What services would I consider? How else might I be helpful?"

General Tips for Using the Stories With Teens or Adults

Reading and discussing a story can help staff and teens gain greater insight into complex issues about becoming independent. Below are discussion questions that can help teens and staff reflect on the issues raised by the stories. In most cases you can read a story and have a discussion in one 45-minute session. At *Represent*, we usually read a story aloud, which takes about 10-15 minutes if you read it straight through. However, it's often very productive to let workshop participants make comments as you go along. The workshop leader may even want to annotate her copy of the story with key questions to prompt discussion at important points.

In starting a discussion after reading the story, we have found that asking a few simple factual questions can break the ice. (Who is the main character? How old is she? What life skill is she struggling with? How did she respond?) Another good starting question is: "What stood out for you in the story?" Go around the room letting each person briefly mention one thing.

You can then move on to open-ended questions, which encourage participants to think more deeply about what the writers were feeling, the choices they faced, and they actions they took. There are no right or wrong answers to the open-ended questions.

Open-ended questions encourage the teens (or staff) in your workshop to think about how the themes, emotions and choices in the stories relate to their own lives. Here are some examples of open-ended questions that we have found to be effective. You can use variations of these questions with almost any story in this book.

- What main problem or challenge did the young person face?

- What choices did the young person have in trying to deal with the challenge?

- Which way of dealing with the challenge was most effective for the young person? Why?

- What strengths, skills, or resources did the young person use or gain? How did the young person gain or learn about those strengths, skills, or resources?

- If you were in the young person's shoes, what would you have done?

- What could adults have done to better help this young person?

- What have you learned by reading this story? What have you learned that you didn't know before?

- What surprised you in this story?

- What, if anything, would you do differently after reading this story?

- Do you have a different view of this issue, or see a different way of dealing with it, after reading this story? Why or why not?

- *For adult staff only*: If you had this young person on your caseload, or in your foster home, what would you have done to assist him or her?

Introduction...from Someone Who's Been There, Done That, and Learned

By RICK BULLARD

Independent living should be run like a military boot camp, because only that kind of tough training is going to prepare us for the stress we'll have in the real world. It's the only way to overcome the false sense of security and dependency the system fosters (no pun intended). We think we're always going to be taken care of, but at 18 (or 21 in New York, where I live) you are out!

Kicked to the Curb

For those who still don't understand, I repeat—at 18 or 21 it's over! Your butt is kicked to the curb like an old pair of sneakers! Outta here like last year!

When I first moved into my independent living facility, I didn't think about that day. I had three more years until I turned 21 and I didn't give a damn about anything, except the money in my pocket.

In my first year there, I pretty much took care of myself. All I did was club, sleep and work. Not a care in the world—no drugs, no booze, just a phunkadelic free-flow of peace and rhythms and grooves.

Soon I was quickly approaching 21 and had begun to realize that the jig was almost up. I should have been saving money, but no one had stressed to me, in a way that would sink in, how important that was. People had told me to save, but not why or how.

So there I was a month before emancipating (or "aging out" as we call it in New York), with no money, no prospects, no future. Not to mention that I also had nowhere to go after discharge. I felt like a deer caught in the headlights of a semi-truck: doomed.

Now I Sleep on the Couch

I grudgingly moved into my mother's one-bedroom apartment and it is here that I currently reside with my mom and my 11-year-old sister.

Oh, and by the way, did I mention I sleep on the couch?

I don't intend to stay here. That's my plan. And that's the whole secret to independent living in the first place—have a plan! Hell, have six damn plans! Just in case your main plan falls through, have backup plans!

I wish I had more of a plan back when I was in independent living. I wish I had learned to save money. I wish I had gotten some sort of on-the-job training, so that I could support myself with a skill. I would have liked to have some sort of housing to look forward to and I wish I had been prepared to go to college.

But none of that happened.

Can You Do Better?

That's why those of us who have been there wrote this book. This book is to help you avoid what happened to me. It's to help you come up with a plan for learning to live independently, and then to stick with it. We named it, "Do You Have What it Takes?" We hope that title scares you a little, 'cause we've learned that's what it takes to properly plan for life after care.

In the following pages writers explore important independent living skills, like making money, getting a job, finding housing, taking care of your health and hygiene, and forming a support network, goals and a plan for leaving care.

Along the way you'll meet a bunch of other former foster youth who have been there, done the aging out thing, struggled, learned, and got though it. They will share their experiences with you so you can avoid making the same mistakes they did.

You'll meet these young adults who wrote about their experiences leaving foster care:

Christine McKenna   **Princess Carr**   **Lenny Jones**

At the end of each chapter you'll find activities and worksheets that will help you prepare for the day you leave foster care. You can work through this book independently, and earn the certificate on p. 307 for successfully completing it. You can also encourage your independent living instructors to use the stories, activites, and worksheets in this book in class.

Now take the quiz on page 21 and find out: Do you have what it takes to make it on your own?

www.youthcomm.org

My First Day Out of Care

The day I was emancipating I didn't really think about it 'cause a lot of other stuff was going on in my life—my grandfather was sick, I had just graduated from high school, and my mind wasn't on emancipation, it was on *now.*

So that day I woke up in a daze. I packed my duffel bag and my foster mother drove me to the Y where I had gotten into a program for youth who had just left care. I unpacked my stuff and sat down. Then I slept that day. When I woke up, I didn't feel anything. There was too much stuff going on to be anything but numb. It didn't really hit me that I was emancipated until a month later. Then it hit me: I fought for five years to be on my own. Now that I had it, did I want it?

Christine McKenna

Test Yourself:
Do You Have What It Takes To Be on Your Own?

By CHRISTINE McKENNA

1. You get your weekly stipend on Friday. You:

a) Put more than half of it in your savings account for when you leave foster care.

b) Spend your stipend paying back everyone you borrowed money from that week.

c) Are broke by midnight because you saw an outfit you just had to have, and a CD you had to get, and, well, you know where I'm going with this.

2. You have one year before you age out of foster care. You need a place to live. You:

a) Start telling everyone you know you're looking for an apartment, apply for Section 8, begin searching the paper to get an idea of what apartments cost, and start thinking about responsible people you might get as roommates.

b) Leave it to fate. You think, "God will find me a home if it's meant to be."

c) Decide you'll move back in with your mom even though every other time you've tried that she's thrown you out in less than a month.

3. When it comes to cooking you:

a) Might as well have your own cooking show. You're so gourmet, people call you Martha Stewart.

b) Try to whip something up every now and then, but end up with visits from the local fire department.

c) Who needs to cook? There's always McDonald's.

4. When you feel lonely you:

a) Call the people you trust and talk to them about how you're feeling.

b) Carry on long and involved debates with Oprah, on TV, whom you consider your close friend.

c) Jump into the first relationship that comes along, fall in love (lust), AWOL to live with your boo, then get kicked out of your sweetie's apartment when his or her "soul mate" returns.

5. Your boss makes a snippy remark to you about your work habits. Your blood boils. You:

a) Calm down, then go to your boss and try to discuss it maturely.

b) Suck it up, then go to a party and drink your weight in vodka.

c) Let your boss have it. Get fired. (Yeah, maybe you should have taken those anger management classes your group home kept giving.)

6. You've been feeling feverish and lightheaded for over a month. You:

a) Head to your doctor. A flu shouldn't last this long!

b) Don't know who your doctor is, so you try every over-the-counter medication there is first.

c) Smoke some pot and forget about it. (If something's wrong with you, you don't want to know.)

7. You finally found an apartment and have left the system. It's time to pay the rent. You:

a) Pay with great joy. It feels so good to be independent!!

b) Ask everyone you know if you can borrow money, even though you probably won't be able to pay them back.

c) Refuse to pay. Your apartment is too small, anyway, and what can they do, throw you out!?

Turn page to see if you're ready!

Scoring

Add up the number of A's, B's and C's you picked. Then read below:

If you answered mostly A's: You are well organized and realistic. Living on your own for the first time isn't easy for anyone, but you will be able to give it your best shot. But make sure to take time out to have fun, too, or you might end up with an ulcer before you can celebrate your first million!

If you answered mostly B's: You take a pretty laid-back approach to life, and tend to put more stock in the zodiac than in your ability to take charge of your destiny. While it's good not to let the world stress you out, keep in mind that becoming independent is no easy feat. The more you plan for your future, the easier it will be. Independent living class is definitely for you.

If you answered mostly C's: You have a devil-may-care attitude toward life and all its responsibilities, and, boy, do you need a wake up call! If you don't get a plan of action for life after foster care soon, you'll spend all your time responding to emergency situations. Trust me, I've been there! I've been planless, jobless and homeless! Don't do things the hard way. Go to independent living class. Make a plan.

Why It's Important to Prepare Now

By JA'NELLE EARLE

Ja'Nelle Earle

When I see TV commercials where a mother has her 3-year-old help sort the laundry, or a father lets his 5-year-old help sweep and mop the floors, I feel angry and sad. Commercials like those remind me of the tiny things parents do to start preparing their children for the real world. They're the things I missed out on growing up in the system. Too often I was babied and I didn't learn how to take care of myself.

Staff at my residential treatment center in San Diego said, "Put your laundry outside your door so it can be washed." In the morning, my laundry would be folded inside my basket, just outside my door.

At the time, I was glad. I didn't like folding clothes. But I never learned to wash my own clothes, so when I left the foster care system, I ruined a lot of clothes by washing them wrong. Like a lot of skills I needed to live independently, I never learned to do it myself.

Too Sheltered by the System

At one group home, I did have to attend an independent living skills program. But once I left that group home to live with my grandmother, it was my choice whether to attend independent living classes or not. No one explained to me that if I didn't learn independent living skills, I would be in trouble when I left the system. Having to sit in a room full of strangers made me nervous, so I just stopped going.

Learning from Mistakes

Now, as a young adult who must be independent at a very early age, I'm trying to catch up. I legally emancipated from the foster care system three years ago. I was not quite finished with high school and had little work experience, which means I couldn't have gotten a well paying job if I wanted to.

www.youthcomm.org

I don't know how I would have found or paid for an apartment to live in. And if I had lived on my own, I'm not sure how I would have dealt with the loneliness of having only myself to count on, or my sometimes overwhelming feelings of anger. Luckily, my grandmother has let me and my son continue living with her. Even so, I still struggle.

When I go grocery shopping, I can't tell you how many times I've bought the name brand item when the generic (no name) brand tastes and looks just the same. I've even lost money not using coupons and not making a shopping list.

I recently purchased a car from my grandmother, and it's been hard paying all the bills for it. Because I never learned about interest rates, when I needed financial assistance I took out a loan without realizing I would have to pay more than I borrowed by the end.

> **Part of being independent is surrounding yourself with a supportive web of people who can help you when you're in trouble.**

A Support Network Helps

Still, I've done better than most of my friends from the foster care system. Some of my peers have tried living with family again, only to be kicked out. Some have become homeless and incarcerated. Many have ended up tied to another system. One girl I know lost her own child to foster care.

Of course, youth leaving care at 18, or even 21, can never be fully prepared to make it on their own without some problems. But the system needs to make sure we have the skills to hold down a job and pay our bills. And youth need to understand that part of being independent is surrounding yourself with a supportive web of people who can help you when you're in trouble.

We youth need to be active about getting all the skills and support we can while we're in care.

Life Skills Start at Home

I try to teach my son life skills even though he's only 3. My son and I clean together, cook together, go shopping together, and I'm even teaching him a little about money. I think it's important to do that with him—learning independent living skills needs to begin at home, wherever that may be.

Activity Page for Group Leaders

Understanding the Need to Prepare for Independence

Topic: What is independent living? Why is it important to plan for the day you leave foster care?

Goal: Help teens understand the importance of planning for the day they leave the system.

Time: 1 hour

Warm-up activity: 10 minutes

■ **Take quiz on page 21.**

■ **Briefly discuss quiz:** Who got the most A's? The most B's? The most C's? What does that mean?

Read and discuss story: 35 minutes

■ **Read story "Why It's Important to Prepare Now" on p. 25.**

■ **Freewrite:** Tell teens that grammar and spelling don't count. The important thing is to get their ideas on the paper. The only rule is that they have to keep their pencils moving, even if they're writing, "I don't know what to write." Read the following prompts out loud and give teens 2 minutes

to respond to each one.

1) What do you think is the scariest thing about living on your own?

2) What will be the best thing about living on your own?

3) How are you preparing to live on your own?

4) Write these skills on a flip chart:

• Experience living in your own apartment

• Good money management skills

• Emotional support and people who can help you in times of trouble

• Job training and work experience

5) Tell the teens about the list: "These are skills and resources that are important to have before leaving foster care. Write a few sentences about which skill seems most important to you, explaining why you think it's vital."

Note: Teens working independently can use the worksheets on p. 31.

■ **Discuss:** Ask for volunteers to read their responses to question #3. Discuss.

Group activity: 15 minutes.

■ **Form Groups:** Divide your group into smaller groups of 2-4 people each.

■ **Give Instructions:** Tell each group that they have to come up with at least three things they think are essential to becoming independent.

For each item on their list, such as "emotional support," they have to write one example of what they mean, such as "I need someone to talk to when I'm lonely." They can include new ideas, as well as things they already do.

■ **Group Work:** Give the teams 5-10 minutes to come up with their lists and sentences.

■ **Share:** Teams read their lists and supporting sentences. If possible, write them on a flip chart.

■ **Discuss:** Have the group discuss which items are most important. (If possible, tell them how their ideas might influence what you do or hope to do in the IL program.)

Think About It

What do you think will the scariest thing about living on your own?

_____

_____

_____

What will be the best thing about living on your own? _____

_____

_____

_____

How are you preparing to live on your own?_____ _____

_____

_____

_____

Below are skills or resources that are important to living on your own. Circle the one that seems most important to you, then write a few sentences about why it seems so important.

Knowing how to rent and keep your own apartment _____

_____

_____

Good money management skills _____

_____

_____

Emotional support and people you can turn to in times of trouble _____

_____

_____

Job training and work experience _____

_____

_____

Chapter 1
Manage That Money

Manage That Money:
Why This Chapter Matters

Princess, now 22, left foster care with absolutely nothing besides the clothes on her back. She went days with no food, money or shelter. She lived in homeless shelters, and even, at times, on the street. Princess feels that part of why she struggled so much was because she had no idea how to save and budget money.

Antwaun Garcia

One mistake Princess made was how she handled her first paycheck, while she was still in care. She had a job as a legal intern and made $4,000. She'd never had that much money in her life. Like many teens who happen to receive a whole chunk of dinero, she didn't know how to handle it.

When people at her agency offered to help Princess open a bank account so she could save, she believed they were trying to steal her money. (They weren't, she now knows.) So her $4,000 lasted only six weeks. Most people could have lived at least three months on that!

After talking with Princess, I realized that all of us teens in care need to learn how to save and budget money before we leave the system.

That's why this chapter is dedicated to money. Yes, money!

You'll learn how to save paper for leaving care. You'll learn how to become a more careful shopper. You'll learn how to avoid credit card hell. You'll also hear about former foster youth who successfully managed their money when they left care. Yes, they do exist!

Lenny, for instance, attended an independent living course that taught him money management skills. Now, he lives in an apartment and is able to work part-time and pay all his bills.

So to all you teens getting ready to leave care, learn how to handle your money now. After interviewing Princess, I know I will!

—Antwaun Garcia

How I Spend

Princess Carr

I'm an impulsive buyer when I do have money, and when I'm broke, I'm broke. I've gone hungry and my lights have been shut off. The cable company came to collect their box. I can't get a phone bill in my name because of my bad credit. I still have no bank account.

How I Save

I am 24 now, and I have a three bedroom apartment. I have roommates to help me cut my rent. So we all pay $335 each instead of me paying a whole G ($1,000) by myself. I figure that all my bills, except my cell phone bill, come to $400 a month. I don't have to bust my ass every day to pay that off.

Lenny Jones

www.youthcomm.org

Mountain Climbing for Beginners

Paying all my bills felt impossible. I learned to take it one step at a time.

By MAYA NOY

I didn't choose to move to Philadelphia, it chose me.

Fresh out of a group home, I visited a friend in Philly and began a part-time job in a small beauty store. I didn't plan on staying there long. But it was a cool job to have. I had never had a "real" job before, other than baby-sitting, but my boss was patient, and I caught on fast.

Alone in My New Apartment

The boss and I got along well, so he told me about a studio apartment that was available close by. That changed my life. I took the apartment, agreed to work full time at the beauty store, and went home to get all my stuff from my mother's house in New York so I could move to Philadelphia.

I remember well that first day that I was really On My Own. It was June 2, 1996. I was only 20, with the maturity (or lack of) to prove it. My mother, the U-HAUL driver and I went to my apartment. My mother and the driver dropped off my things—which took about 30 minutes—and then left. I was alone in my own apartment, with a mess of my belongings around me, in a town I didn't really know.

A rush of overwhelming loneliness hit me very hard and suddenly, and all I could do was stare at my disorganized possessions that reminded me of being home. I couldn't help but just sit there and cry. Who could I call when I was lonely or bored? Who would I talk to for hours to fill the silence? Long distance calls weren't cheap back then! Who would I turn to when I needed help? Who would I hang out with on weekends? I was no longer excited by the prospect of being all grown up and independent.

One Step at a Time

Maybe half an hour of crying passed before I realized that I was in the real world now, with no one to wipe my tears but me. So that's what I did. I made up my mind right then and there to grow up and deal with my new life.

As I unpacked and organized my place, I began to get excited again. I was on my own! No one to tell me what to do or when to come home or how to clean up!

That excitement didn't last long either. It took me about a week to get my place to look the way I wanted it to.

And as I fixed up my apartment, I had to start thinking about food, getting a phone hooked up, finding laundry facilities, opening a bank account so I could save money from my job, and more. And that was only the beginning.

It all seemed so overwhelming at first. I had to learn how to take it one step at a time. That's advice I would give to anyone just starting out on their own: One step at a time, and it won't look like such a tall mountain to climb.

> **Despite all the things that I went through, I've always enjoyed feeling grown up and independent.**

I was able to get some start-up money from my mother, I paid back monthly. I budgeted carefully, and tried not to spend money if I didn't absolutely have to. I saved on transportation expenses since my job was next door, and I wore a uniform to work, so that saved money for clothes. I didn't get luxuries such as cable, a cell phone, or a car, so I ended up doing fairly well handling my bills. And the rent in Philadelphia wasn't too high, so I didn't have to beg, borrow or steal.

Still, I did struggle making sure that I worked enough hours to cover all my expenses—rent, food, electricity and the phone bill. I was always afraid I would get sick, and be out of a day's pay. If so, I would have had trouble paying for all my expenses that first year, when I hadn't started saving money yet. But somehow I always managed to keep my head above water. I didn't get sick and I don't think there was ever a time I was late with a payment.

Getting the Hang of It

After a few years, I felt like I was getting the hang of paying bills and being on my own.

I didn't get a credit card, which allows you to spend money you don't even have as long as you pay back more than you spend. Whenever possible, I washed clothes by hand to avoid the laundromat. So I began to save money here and there.

I still hadn't made many good friends in my new life, but I didn't mind. I had gotten used to being alone and I actually liked it.

But I did encounter one major problem. That was the heat, which was supposed to come with my apartment. It was the dead of winter, and I was getting no heat at all. And no one cared!

I called the landlord, who agreed to fix it, but never did. I even tried calling the Health Department, but I didn't see any results there either. I called the Housing Department, but had the worst time getting through. I even tried to get legal assistance, but I was too shy, and had trouble telling my story in a way that people would want to help me. They didn't have patience for me and how I stumbled over my words.

I didn't know how to get the right person to pay attention to me and solve this problem. I still have an entire stuffed and tattered folder filled with all my efforts to resolve this. None worked.

This problem had me very frustrated, and deeply depressed. And I was freezing! I had pet turtles that died because it was too cold. So I took my landlord to court to give me heat. I was a shy, 20-something female, without legal representation. The judge and my landlord were friends. The result? I had to settle for a space heater (which I had to buy myself) and wear more clothes at night to keep warm.

Eventually the landlord was replaced with a new landlord who is more helpful. I still have problems with the heat now and then, but it's not as bad. His excuse is, "It's an old building, so deal with it." So I do. But I still think about getting justice for the past. (Except I'm still not sure how to go about it!)

Dealing with a difficult landlord and making ends meet on my own, I

$

have had to grow up quickly. That's been good. It's now seven years and several jobs later since I first moved to Philadelphia. I now do clerical work, like answering phones and typing, at an audio visual company. I have even been making extra money by renting out a room in my new apartment. Now I'm able to save more and more.

All Grown Up

I am also much better at standing up for myself and getting help when I need it. I am still working on learning to express myself. I found that when I feel someone is treating me unfairly (a landlord, a boss, the phone company) it is easier for me to write than to verbally confront someone in person or on the phone. Knowing this about myself helps me get what I need more often. (And sometimes writing works best because no one answers the phone these days!)

Being on your own, there's always something to overcome, but I have to say that whatever fear I felt at first slowly dissolved. I am proud of myself for being able to survive, and not run home to Mommy. And despite all the things that I went through, I've always enjoyed feeling grown up and independent.

In some ways living on your own doesn't get any easier, but you get so caught up in it, that you don't even realize how hard it is. It's like climbing that mountain—if you look at the mountain it feels overwhelming, but if you just focus on the step ahead of you, chances are you'll get to the top.

How to Save Paper

By ANTWAUN GARCIA

In foster care, a lot of your bills are paid for. When you leave care, chances are that you're going to need to support yourself. You need to

Antwaun Garcia

have money saved up in case of an emergency. God forbid you get laid off from your job and you don't have money saved, you'll be in trouble. You won't have that check to rely on, so the bills will be piling up and the pressure will be on you. But you wouldn't be in that situation if you'd saved. (And nowadays finding a job is harder than losing weight.)

So now, every time you get paid, put some of it away to save, even if it is just a small amount.

1. Open a Bank Account. A bank is the best place to save money, because if you hide your money at home and someone finds it, or the house burns down, or you forget where you hid it, you're in trouble. Besides, once your money's in the bank, it's more likely to stay there.

2. Be a Careful Shopper. David Bradshaw, who works at Citibank in New York City, explained that when he was a teen, he had trouble saving money because he always wanted to rock the latest gear. "I couldn't save a dime," he said. "I had to have the Jordan's and the long chain with the stones. My first week after getting a check it was gone. The second week I went right back to feeding off my mother and grandmother. That shouldn't be the case. You should know how to budget your money."

The moral of the story: Just because you have money don't mean you have to spend it. A lot of us teens spend way too much money to have the latest gear. You can still be hip, keep up with the dress code, and save.

When you do shop, try to estimate what everything will cost so you don't spend more than you want to. To save more money, don't buy brand names. Instead of buying Colgate toothpaste, for instance, buy the drug store brand, which is going to be less expensive. If you know you use a lot of shampoo, buy the bigger size if you can afford it. It usually costs less in the long run to buy supplies in bigger amounts.

3. Avoid Credit Cards. To make a long story short, credit cards make it easy to spend a bunch of money you don't have…and then you owe even more! Before you know it, you'll have the credit card companies knocking on your door and threatening to make your life miserable.

4. Learn How to Budget. Learn how to budget your money. To budget, write down how much money you make each month. Then figure out how much you must spend each month on essentials like deodorant, transportation and rent. Subtract how much you spend each month from how much you make each month. What you have left over is how much you can use to buy extra stuff… but make sure you save some of it!

Confessions of a Shopaholic

My biggest fetish is probably shoes. I used to buy a new pair every two weeks. My worst mistake was a pair of lime green, suede hush puppies that I bought for 105 bucks! But I really shouldn't single out shoes because I'm just a compulsive shopaholic.

I once blew my paycheck and more in a cosmetics store so I could decorate my dresser. I was depressed and Byron, my shopping buddy, tried to do everything in his power to cheer me up. Nothing was really helping. But when he said shopping, I suddenly had a burst of energy.

When I shop I feel like I'm on top of the world. My eyes get sort of wide because of all the things I see that I want, and I don't really look at the price tags. I just get so excited to be buying things that I don't really care how much they cost.

It's not a problem right now, because I have a job and not a lot of expenses, but if I don't learn to slow down, being a shopaholic might be a big problem in the future—like when I age out of the foster care system.

—Jeremiyah Spears

Saving for My Future

For kids like me, trying to figure out life at 18 is a little nerve-wracking. At 18 you are considered an adult, so you have to realize that being a kid is over and depending on others for a lot of things must stop. To me, that's a good feeling, but getting ready for independence is important, because it's also scary.

Scott Burke

I started a bank account when I was 14 (with a little help from some girl's mother who worked at a bank). When I first started I opened an account for kids, because I only had to put in $20 to start. Then I started to save money every time I got it. If I had five dollars I would save a dollar out of it.

I also started working a job at my group home campus, when I was 12. My job was to wake up at 6 a.m. to hand out papers to each of the 30 cottages. The job paid $2.25 every hour and I left the group home with $250 saved.

Then, through my city's Summer Youth Employment Program, I got a job a hospital as a maintenance worker. From there I finally got a job as a medical librarian. That gave me experience I could use for a well-paying career. Through this job I learned a lot about medicine and what goes on in the hospital.

Eventually, I opened a regular account and transferred my savings into it.

Saving money and working my way up to jobs with more responsibility made me feel good. I liked knowing that I was getting my life started and becoming self-sufficient. It made me feel grown and responsible.

—Scott Burke

Shopping Smart

By JEREMIYAH SPEARS and SHAHIM SCOTT

Kerrie Toole, a social work intern at Green Chimneys, a group home in New York City, is also a student without a lot of money to throw around. Here's how she makes a little money go a long way.

Why do you budget your money?

Answer: Because I have no income right now, and only $1,000 to my name. Plus, I'm in debt by $60,000 for college loans, and I'll need to pay back $600 each month after I graduate from social work school.

How did you get into so much debt?

Answer: I'm going to graduate school and schools have to be paid, so I had to take out loans. School's expensive, but I think it's worth living on a budget for now because in the end I'm going to be getting a higher paying job because I went to school. I'm going to be a social worker.

How much do you spend a month?

Answer: I spend $523 a month on rent, but that's paid for by my loans. Out of my own savings I spend about $60 a month on transportation, $50 to $60 a month on food, and about $50 a month on my telephone bill. That leaves me about $100 a month for savings or any extras I might need.

How do you decide what's necessary for you to have and what's not?

Answer: The necessary things are the basics. I have very basic makeup—one mascara, chapstick, cover-up, moisturizer. That's it. My clothes are basic—mostly jeans and shirts that I bought on sale. And I'm too busy with school to have much entertainment. I watch TV at home, and that's free, because I don't have cable.

I eat dinner out once a month, because eating out once can cost as much as I'd normally spend for an entire week. Otherwise I spend $20 to $30 every two weeks on food. I eat lots of pastas and rice because those are the cheapest foods and they are filling. A dinner of pasta and sauce can cost only $2. I also buy chicken or pork and stick it in the freezer for later, and usually I eat a little vegetables on the side. Sometimes it does get tiring to eat these foods. If I had money I'd have salmon.

Do you have a system for finding the lowest prices?

Answer: When you're shopping for things you need you can compare prices, and buy the cheaper things. Usually the store brand is very similar to the name brand product but it costs less.

I go to the store with a limit in my head. I'll say, "I'm only going to spend $20 and that's it." In the store, I do the math in my head before I get to the check-out so I know I don't over-spend.

Think About It

How do you spend your money? _____

_____

_____

_____

_____

What do you buy that you *need*? _____

_____

_____

_____

_____

_____

What do you buy that you *don't* need? _____

_____

_____

_____

_____

_____

What things could you spend less money on or do without to start saving money?

_____

_____

_____

_____

www.youthcomm.org

Credit Card Hell

I shopped 'til I dropped...into debt.

By XAVIER REYES

My debt problems started when I went to college and got my first credit card. I was 17 years old and I was still living in a group home. Just

Xavier Reyes

like every other college freshman, I was bombarded with credit card applications in the mail. Since I had two part-time jobs, I figured that if I got a credit card and used it to buy the things I needed, I would be able to pay the bills when they arrived.

So I applied, not for one credit card, but for three. As luck would have it, I got approved for all three. I felt more like an adult. I could buy things and not have to pay for them 'til later.

As soon as my credit cards arrived in the mail, I signed the back of them and headed off to shop. At that time I was going through an Adidas clothes phase. I had sneakers, pants, shirts, shorts, headbands, wristbands, two coats and even a book bag that was from Adidas.

With my credit card, I bought even more Adidas stuff as well as CDs, a radio and video games. It was amazing. I didn't have to have the money to buy these things. I could just give the store owners any one of my three credit cards and whatever I wanted was mine.

Three Credit Cards

While the credit limits on each of these cards were $700 each—which means I could spend up to $700 with each one—I managed to spend that amount on the cards quickly. When the bills came in, I paid the minimum amount that was due, which wasn't more than $25 per card.

I thought that as long as I paid this minimum amount and paid it on time each month I would be fine. I didn't know then how credit cards worked. I didn't know that even though I paid the minimum due, the credit cards still took a percentage of the rest of the money I owed, and added that to the amount I owed. This is how credit card companies earn money.

For instance, say you owe $400. Even if you pay the minimum amount due and don't use the credit card to buy anything else, the next month you will owe more than $400, because they charge you interest on what you still owe. Believe it or not, it might not be long before the $400 you owe has turned into $800.

How Can I Pay Them?

My own bills skyrocketed. Soon I owed $1,800 to the credit card companies. I felt I could not handle the bills, like I was trying to climb out of a deep hole, but the more I tried to get out of it, the slippier it was.

At first I wanted to be responsible and keep my credit cards in good standing. So I paid what I could afford. After a while, though, I got tired of paying bills altogether. I wanted to spend my money on myself, not on my creditors. I began to miss payments. When I missed a payment, a late fee would be added to my credit card bill, which could cost a lot—one card charged $25 a month if I didn't pay the minimum balance on time! How was I ever going to pay that back?

I reached a point where I thought there was no way I could pay my credit cards back. So I went from making late payments to making no payments at all. I hoped that somehow they would all just disappear, that they would pay themselves off.

But they never did.

Warning Letters

I got letter after letter from the creditors telling me that if I did not pay them back it would affect my credit rating. This meant they would write up a report saying I was not good at paying back loans. That could make my future hard for me, because often when you're trying to rent an apartment or buy a home or borrow money for college, they check your credit rating to see if you are good at paying back money. If you were lousy at paying back your credit cards, you won't get the apartment or the loan—or you may have to pay more for it.

I grew concerned. When I left foster care, I wanted to have my own apartment. I knew that in order to have this, I had to have good credit. There were also other things that I wanted—like a car and, one day, a house. The only way I was going to be able to repair my credit was to pay the bills that I ignored for so long.

$2,100 in the Hole

So I started paying them. Or at least I thought I was doing so.

Turns out that because I had allowed the late charges and penalties to pile up on the bills, I was way over my $700 credit limit. So I was also now paying an over-the-limit-fee, which is different from a late charge. The over-the-limit-fee was $25 a month for each month I was over-the-limit. This meant that each month, even if I didn't buy anything with my credit cards, I could be charged a $25 late fee, plus a $25 over-the-limit fee, plus interest on all the things I had bought.

At this point, I now owed the credit card companies thousands of dollars. I had definitely gotten myself into a hole and I was having a hard time getting out.

I began paying as much as I could—which was about $50 per card—but no matter how much I paid, it seemed like I just kept owing more money.

Finally, to my relief, I heard about a debt management agency that could take all my bills and work with my creditors to give me lower interest rates for the amounts I owed. This would make it easier to keep up with my debt, and would also help stop the annoying letters and phone calls that I was getting about my bills, as long as I paid the lower rates reliably. Also, instead of making five separate payments, I would now make only one payment to the debt management agency, and then they would pay my creditors.

Trying to Break Free

To this day, five years later, I am still paying off the credit cards. Right now I owe about $1,000 in credit cards. I have cut up all my cards except for one, so that I will not keep spending money that I don't have. I decided to keep that one credit card just in case I have an emergency.

Now it's a burden to have to carry these bills so many years later, especially since I now live on my own. After I get done paying the rent, utilities, phone bill, cable, buying food, paying for transportation, paying what I owe to the credit cards and other bills, I barely have $50 left to myself.

Paying for My Misspent Youth

In addition, my credit is now messed up. Had I known that negative items stay on my credit report for seven years (yes, seven years!), I would have thought twice about not paying the bills back. I still want a house and a car, but if I don't clean up the mess I made when I was younger, it will never happen.

Now I truly resent credit cards. I look at them as a trap, baited with everything your heart desires (or that your credit limit allows). It's a pain in the butt to have to pay bills from when I was younger. And just to think, I don't even wear Adidas anymore.

Activity Page for Group Leaders

Learning to Budget

Topic: Learning to budget.

Goal: Help make teens aware of the expenses involved in living independently and how to make informed spending choices.

Time: 1 hour and 15 minutes.

What you'll need: Enough copies of the help wanted and apartment rental sections of your local newspaper for every two people in your group.

An estimate of what the following services cost each month in your area: cable TV; electricity for a one-bedroom apartment; local phone service; heat and hot water; transportation.

1) Warm-up discussion: 10-15 minutes.

■ **Tell teens:** "Imagine you are moving into your first apartment. You already have a job, but you don't have a lot of money. You know that to pay the bills you will need to be very careful about how you spend your money. Some things you may decide to do without—like cable TV. Other things you absolutely need in your first apartment, like electricity. What must you absolutely have in your first apartment? What would you like in your apartment but could live without if you needed to?"

■ **List the items on the board.** At this point, it's not important to have a complete list of everything your group will need to set up an apartment.

■ **Have teens estimate the monthly cost of each item.**

■ **Leave the list on the board.**

2) Read story: 15-20 minutes.

■ **Tell teens:** "We're going to read a story out loud about a young woman in foster care who moves into her own apartment for the first time. Every time she lists an expense that we haven't already mentioned, point it out and we'll add it to our own list and estimate its cost per month."

■ **Taking turns, read out loud "Mountain Climbing for Beginners" by Maya Noy on page 36.**

■ **As you read, pause to list the expenses Maya mentions that aren't already on the board, and estimates their monthly cost.**

3) Group activity: 30 minutes

■ **Divide group into pairs.**

■ **Pass out classified section of your local newspaper.**

■ **Tell group:** "Pretend that you are officially on your own. Each team needs to act as one person. From the classified section, you need to find a job that you are qualified for and that you can live on. For instance, you can't take a typing job if you don't know how to type. You will also need to find an apartment you can afford on your job.

"The team that does the best job of planning a life that they can afford wins. You should strive to save a little money each month, so that you have something to fall back on in case of emergencies."

■ **Help teams estimate their monthly pay:** Circulate around the room as teams pick their jobs and apartments from the classifieds. Help teens estimate how much the job will pay them each month so they can make sure they have enough money for their rent. For instance, if the job has a yearly salary, they should divide that salary by 12 months to find the monthly income. If the job doesn't list a salary, and does not require a high school degree, assume it is minimum wage. The worksheet on p. 54 helps teens calculate their income for hourly wage.

■ **After everyone has chosen an apartment, and found their monthly salary, tell teens:** "Now choose from the board the items that you absolutely cannot live without in your new life. Then add up the monthly cost of those things. These will be your monthly expenses. Make sure you can afford them on your salary. If you can't, you can choose a new job, a cheaper apartment, or do without one of the expenses. You can also rent a room in an apartment you will share with others to save money." The worksheet on p. 55 helps teens calculate this.

4) Debate: 10 -15 minutes

(If you don't have time to get to this debate, collect the teams' budget plans and save this part of the lesson until your next meeting)

■ **Give each team 2-3 minutes to present their plan:** Have each team present their monthly budget, explaining the expenses they decided they could and could not live without. Feel free to question each group to get teams to thoroughly explain their choices or if something in their budget seems unrealistic. For instance, it is unlikely that they will want to do without electricity to save money.

■ **Pick a winner:** After the groups have presented their budgets, choose the team which has made the most sound, realistic budget in your opinion, and explain why. It is a good idea to pick a team that manages to save a little bit of money each month, even if it is only $5.

My Budget

CALCULATE YOUR MONTHLY PAY: *Imagine you are moving into your first apartment. Look in the job listings of your local newspaper or online, like Craig's List if your town has one, and pick a job you are qualified for that tells how much it pays. Estimate how much it will let you make per month using this formula:*

Monthly pay = pay per hour x number of hours worked a week x 4 weeks in a month

EXAMPLE:

If your job pays $10 an hour for 20 hours a week, you will make:

$10 x 20 hours a week x 4 weeks per month =

$800 pay per month before taxes.

> WARNING! You will be taxed at least $15 for every $100 you make. So if you make $800, you will be taxed at least $15 x 8 = $120. This means that if you earn $800 you will take home $680 ($800 − $120).

Calculate the monthly pay you will take home in the space below.

My monthly pay: $_____

IDENTIFY YOUR NEEDS: *To pay your bills you will need to be very careful you don't spend more money than you earn. Ideally, you will even make enough money so that you can save a bit each month, so you will have money saved for an emergency, like if you lose your job or miss a few days of work due to getting sick.*

To make sure you don't spend more than you earn, you may decide to do without some things—like cable TV. These are things you may want but don't need.

Other things you may feel you absolutely need in your first apartment, like electricity. These are your needs.

List all the things you need in your apartment. We have started the list for you:

THINGS I NEED:	APPROXIMATE COST PER MONTH
Rent	
Electricity and gas (if it's not included in rent)	
Transportation	
Groceries	
Phone service	
TOTAL COST PER MONTH	

www.youthcomm.org

IDENTIFY YOUR WANTS: *List all the things you want in your apartment, but don't need. These are the things you'd like to have but can live without. We have started the list for you, but feel free to cross items out!*

THINGS I WANT:	APPROXIMATE COST PER MONTH
Cable TV	
Lifesize poster of Chuck Norris	
Cute cat for company (including cat food, vet bills, litter for the litter box)	
Playstation	
TOTAL COST PER MONTH	

Now go back to your "Things I Need" list and write down how much they will cost per month. Consult your local newspaper's apartment listings or Craig's List if your town has one for ideas about how much rent costs. (Remember, sharing an apartment cuts down on rent!)

Add up your total cost per month of needs. This is the amount you will need to spend each month, no matter what!

Write your total take home pay per month here:　　　　$_____

Write the total you need to spend per month here:　　— $_____

TOTAL PAY MINUS TOTAL YOU NEED TO SPEND EQUALS:　$_____

This is the amount you can spend on your wants. If your number is negative, you need to make more money or find ways to spend less money on your needs, like by finding a cheaper place to live.

Chapter 2
On the Job

On the Job:
Why This Chapter Matters

Finding a job isn't easy. Keeping one can be challenging, as well. In this chapter teens and former foster youth write about the challenges of finding a job and learning how to get along with cranky coworkers, domineering bosses, and difficult customers. You'll also find practical tips for acing a job interview and holding onto that paycheck once you've got it.

Finding a Job I Love

Keeping a job ain't hard, depending on what kind of job. I've had jobs that I just did for the money, and usually I got fired for coming in late. That's why now I don't do jobs that have a strict schedule. Once I found a job that I actually liked—which was being a sex education and alcohol peer counselor—I kept it. It was a good job for the simple fact that I could work just about anywhere. If I didn't like working at one place I could go back to the agency that got me trained and say I wanted to work somewhere else, and they'd ask for my resume and send me somewhere else. It didn't pay a lot, but I loved doing it and it paid the bills.

Lenny Jones

Leave Your Problems at Home

I've got a lot of issues that I'll live with for the rest of my life, but I know that when I'm on a job, my problems can't get in the way. You can't be depressed on your job, you have to work.

Princess Carr

www.youthcomm.org

Getting My First Job Was a Pain in the Butt!

By DANIELLE WILSON

A while ago, all of my friends had jobs and I didn't. That's because they had a "hook up." (In case you don't know, a "hook up" is when a person who has a job gets you one with no problem.)

At times, I wished I had a hook up! If I did, I wouldn't have had to go through all those nervous interviews, or waste my ink on those applications that probably got thrown in the trash. If I had a dollar for every time I filled out an application, I wouldn't need a job!

Danielle Wilson

No Experience

My job search really started when I turned 16. I went from store to store and filled out applications back to back. One day I asked my grandmother, "Why does no one want to hire me?" She said it was because I didn't have any experience.

How was I supposed to have experience when I'd never had a job before? McDonald's wouldn't even hire me. I applied there so many times it was a shame.

The Gap was one of the hardest places to apply. Once you fill out an application, the managers interview you right on the spot. It made me so nervous that I couldn't talk right.

A Tough Question

The first question they ask is, "Why do you want to work for the Gap?" Your mind is telling you to say: "For the money, dummy." But you don't want to say that because you don't want to make yourself sound greedy, even if it's the truth.

So I'd say, "Because I'm familiar with what the company does. Which is sell clothes." (Doesn't the interview sound good so far?)

Yes, but not for long because there was this one question that always seemed to get me every time: "What can you bring to this company?"

I don't know, maybe more customers?

Every time they asked me that question, my heart would stop and drop all the way to the floor. By the time I got ready to pick it up, I heard them say, "If we don't contact you in 24 hours, you didn't get the job."

I don't know about any of you, but to me that question is hard to answer. I got the impression that the manager wanted me to say a certain thing.

Like, there's one right answer and if I get it wrong, I've failed.

But if I was asked that question now, I would say, "I'm a hard worker and a very reliable person, and with those kinds of abilities I cannot only do a good job, but I can influence other employees to do so too."

One time I was so close to getting a job at Burger King. My friend Cindy, who was supposed to be my "hook up," told her manager that she had a friend who wanted to work there.

So I went down, filled out an application, and handed it to the manager personally. He called me two days later and told me to come down the next day and bring my working papers, Social Security card and a picture ID.

> **If I had a dollar for every time I filled out an application, I wouldn't need a job!**

'I Got the Job'

I was so excited when he called, I started jumping up and down screaming, "Grandma, I got the job, I got the job!" Like I won the lottery or something.

The next day I went down there early for my interview. The manager was in a meeting, so he sent the assistant manager to interview me. (Mind you, she was new.)

An Age Problem

During the interview the assistant manager was asking me simple stuff that I could answer on the drop of a dime. Then she asked, "How old are you?"

"Sixteen, miss."

"Oh, I'm sorry, you have to be 16 and a half to work here."

I exploded. "Why do you have to be 16 and a half?" I said in a not-so-nice tone.

> **How was I supposed to have experience when I'd never had a job before?**

She said, "Because you have to work with a grill and hot oil."

"But what does being 16 and a half got to do with it?"

"Because…" she tried to say.

"I don't want to hear it, miss. That doesn't make any sense. Can I please speak to the manager?" I yelled.

"You'll have to wait until he gets out of the meeting."

"Then I'll wait," I said.

So I waited a half an hour, watching the assistant manager interview other people, including my other friend Shantel. She got the job with no problems, because she was 17.

When the manager came out I immediately went toward him and asked, "How old do you have to be to work here?"

"Sixteen," he said.

"Why did the assistant manager tell me that I have to be 16 and a half?"

Group Interview

"I didn't tell her that," the assistant manager said. "I put a question mark on her application because she attends school in the day and you told me you were taking people that could work during the day."

"Oh, you're right," the manager said. And he walked out of the store before I could tell him that my friend got hired and goes to school. I looked at the lady and rolled my eyes.

But after I thought about it, I realized that I shouldn't have yelled and acted like I did. That was very unprofessional. I should have just left it alone, said, "Thank you," and walked away.

During the holidays, I tried Gap again. I answered all the manager's questions. My heart was going to drop, but I held onto it.

After the interview I got kind of excited because the manager said, "OK," took out a piece of paper, handed it to me and said, "You have a group interview on the 2nd of December at 4:30. Be there a half-hour early." My heart made a complete stop.

A group interview is when you're not the only one getting interviewed. The manager interviews several people at the same time.

I was kind of disappointed because I thought I was going to be hired on the spot. But another part of me was excited because I had never gotten this far with the Gap before.

Picking an Outfit

On the day of the group interview I got there an hour early. I know, I was desperate, but it's good to get there early.

By the time 4:30 came, there were eight girls including myself. Well, to me the interview was fun. The manager gave each of us a card and we had to pretend that we worked there and were picking out an outfit for the person described on the card.

My person was a female looking for an outfit to wear for a date. She didn't want anything loose or baggy, and she didn't want anything in denim.

So I picked out a black skirt and a black dressy shirt and a little handbag. During the interview we had to describe the outfits we picked and why. Then the manager asked us some questions and the interview was over. She told us that if we didn't get called for a third interview, then try again next year.

Third interview?! What do they think, working at the Gap is a career? I didn't get called.

But I learned, through McDonald's and the Gap, that a lot of jobs are very hard to get. And despite all the bad luck I seemed to have, I didn't give up. Eventually, I finally found a summer job.

It's a Start

There was a summer job program in New York City that I never knew about while I was applying at fast food restaurants. If you live in a housing project like myself, you may qualify. You have to do almost everything, like keeping the projects clean. (I don't mind being in the sun; I need a tan.)

I know some of you are thinking, "I'm not cleaning up for nobody." I was thinking the same way. But hey, it paid minimum wage and it was a job. And cleaning isn't that bad!

Besides, you have to start at the bottom before you reach the top. And the next time I looked for a job, it was that much easier. I already had work experience.

Job Hunting
Words From the Wise

If you're looking for a job,
tell everyone you know that you're looking.
Tell people at church, school—somebody
might know somebody who might be in a position
to give you a job.

—Tom Pendleton, Executive Director
New York Citywide School to Work Alliance

How to Ace Your Job Interview

By XAVIER REYES

Okay, picture this—you just got your first job interview, right, and all of a sudden a whole bunch of questions start popping into your mind:

Xavier Reyes

"What do I say?"

"What should I wear?"

"What papers should I bring?"

"What time is the best time to be there?"

Have no fear! This article will help answer the questions of you first-time job interviewees.

Now, there are a few important things you must remember:

1. Have Your Documents. Before you go on the interview, make sure that you have the following documents (by the way, it's almost impossible to get a job without them):

☐ Birth certificate

☐ Social Security card

☐ Immunization record

☐ Working papers

☐ Some, but not all jobs, like you to have a resume (a list of your previous jobs and work experience)

2. Be On Time. Never be late to the interview. That suggests that you are irresponsible, and that's not a good first impression to make. In fact, show up at least 10 minutes early for your interview. (If you run into transportation trouble and are going to be late, call the interviewer to let her know.)

3. Be Polite. Don't use slang or street talk when talking to the interviewer. There's a time and place for slang and a time and place for standard English. For example, don't greet the interviewer by saying,

"What's poppin', son?" Instead, say, "Hello, thank you for interviewing me."

4. Dress to Impress. Please, please don't walk into the
interviewer's office with a pair of jeans and a white tee. I don't think the interviewer will hire someone who looks like they're getting ready to go to a party. It doesn't hurt to be too dressed up. It can hurt to be too casual.

So men should wear a white shirt, maybe even a tie, a dark jacket, dark pants or khakis and shoes (no sneakers). Women should wear a white blouse, a skirt or nice pants, and dress shoes (no super-high heels). (Don't worry, the interview won't last more than an hour.)

5. Look 'Em In the Eyes. Try to look the interviewer in
the eyes when you are talking and listening to her. If you're looking away while you're answering a question, it will seem like you don't have good social skills. And don't chew gum!

6. Listen and Show Interest. Listen carefully to what
the interviewer is saying and ask questions about the job. (You might want to find out some information about the company or store before you go on the interview.) Asking questions shows that you are really enthusiastic about the job. These are some good questions to ask:

☐ What will I do on the job?

☐ What is a typical day like?

☐ Do I need any type of degree, diploma or recommendations to get this job?

☐ What are the hours?

☐ Is there room for advancement?

☐ How much is the pay?

7. Say a Proper Goodbye. Always, always shake the hand
of the interviewer at the beginning and the end of the interview. It's a form of respect. As soon as you get home, write a thank you letter to the interviewer. If you haven't heard from the interviewer in three or four days, call her and see what's up with the job!

You're Fired!

Losing eight jobs has taught me a lot.

By CHRISTINE McKENNA

As a teen, I never had the luxury of an after-school job. I know that some kids in foster care are allowed to have part-time jobs, but the

Christine McKenna

group home I lived in was very iffy about letting the girls work. It was one of those double-edged sword situations: if you were acting up and an emotional wreck, of course they wouldn't let you work. But if you were a good little resident and followed all the rules, they didn't want to jeopardize that by letting you work. Catch-22.

That's why I didn't work at all until I was 18 and had aged out of foster care in Los Angeles. I had no idea how difficult it would be to find a job, let alone keep it. Let's see, I'm 23 now, and I've had about eight different jobs, but from each one I've learned something valuable. Here are four of the main lessons I learned.

Lesson of Job #1: Take It Easy, Chica!

My first job was as a secretary at a law firm in Brentwood, California. I answered phones, typed, faxed, emailed clients and did just about anything else asked of me. I worked full time, Monday through Friday. I was also going to college full-time at Santa Monica College. I then decided, because I wanted the extra cash, to get a part-time job for the weekends. I ended up working at a clothing department store as the person who hung up the clothes you shoppers (you know who you are) leave strewn all over the dressing room. So basically, I was working 60 hours a week, plus attending school full-time in the evening.

Well, as you can imagine, I was working way too much. And it didn't take long for me to literally pass out from sheer exhaustion at school one night. I had to be hospitalized from the stress, and I ended up losing both jobs.

The lesson learned here is: Take it easy, chica! Running at full sprint all the time will kill you.

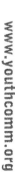

In a weird way, I was relieved to lose those jobs. I was burning myself out, but I didn't know how to stop myself. I didn't know my own limitations at the time, or how to really protect myself from working too hard. I needed to learn to pace myself.

Lesson of Job #2: Even if Your Boss Is Super Cute and Cool, He (or She) Is Your Boss in the Office, Not Your Friend

Soon after this I found employment at a nonprofit group that taught the arts to kids.

I was an administrative assistant, which I learned was just a fancy term for gofer. I basically did the same things I did at the law firm, along with numerous errands. I loved this job intensely, mostly because it was run by two of the cutest guys ever, Tim and Jason.

I thought I'd become really good friends with Tim and Jason, although thinking back on it, how good of a friend can an 18-year-old be to two guys in their 30's? Whatever the case, I felt close to them and I saw myself as the "fun" of the office. I liked to have everyone laughing. Sometimes to make people laugh, I'd say really inappropriate things, like sexual things. You get the picture.

But it turns out, those kind of comments aren't OK in a work environment, not even if you are good friends with the bosses. They are especially not OK when you're working with kids.

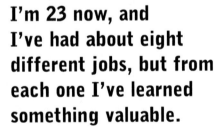

I'm 23 now, and I've had about eight different jobs, but from each one I've learned something valuable.

I knew these things, but I didn't pay attention to what I knew. I think it was because I got too chummy with my employers, and that confused me. Being that close to your co-workers creates really fuzzy boundaries, and I forgot what's appropriate office behavior and what is not. It was hard for me to tell the difference between Tim and Jason my bosses, and Tim and Jason my friends. Because Tim and Jason were my friends, I forgot that maybe it's not appropriate to be talking in the office about the guy I was debating whether or not to sleep with.

So after working there for a little over a year, I lost that job too. That hurt. I still really miss that job. If Tim and Jason were to call me today and give me another chance working for them, I would be there in an instant.

Lesson of Job #3: Get Along With Your Boss, Even if You Can't Stand the Jerk

My next job was at Staples, where I made copies for people who were too lazy to do it themselves. I worked mornings at Staples and went to school in the evenings. I literally dreamed of paper jams and colored paper for weeks!

A lot of customers came in again and again and it was nice getting to know them. I liked talking to the customers.

But I didn't like my boss, and I didn't like it that many people were very impatient and couldn't seem to understand that the sentence, "There's nothing I can do, the machine is broken," means exactly that.

Other than that, it was a decent job.

But this story wouldn't be good without me saying that, yes, I also lost this job. This time it was because I accidentally signed the wrong name for a FedEx package. Could happen to anyone. I don't think my manager thought so, though. Since we never really got along, I feel like he had been looking for an excuse to fire me. The FedEx package was his excuse, and I was jobless again.

The lesson I learned from this job is to make an effort to get along with your boss, even if you can't stand him or her.

Lesson of Job #4: Know Your Limits and Set Boundaries to Protect Them

The next job (God I'm getting tired of saying that) was as a receptionist at a company that sold knives. This was actually a pretty cool gig, until once again (I don't seem to learn my lessons well!) I immersed myself so entirely in the job that I no longer had a life outside of work. I was pulling something like 80 hours a week, and only getting paid for 40.

Why? By this time I think I was so desperate not to lose another job that I went to great lengths to be the best damn employee there ever was. I would come in at 6 in the morning to get a jumpstart on returning calls and to straighten up the interview room. Sometimes I wouldn't leave until

11 at night, cleaning up the office, vacuuming and such, and listening to my boss' personal problems.

Not only was I afraid of getting fired, but I was avoiding being at home. By this time, I was living in an apartment with people I hated. The way I saw it, the less time spent there the better, so I spent all my time at work.

Feeling Needed and Useful

But the job was draining me. And so was my boss, who sometimes asked me to lie to clients. I hate to lie. And soon my boss was telling me all his problems—personal and otherwise. I listened compassionately and offered what little advice I could. To be honest, I liked being the go-to-girl for him. It made me feel needed and useful, so once again I did not set clear boundaries with my boss.

What I did not like was the sleepless nights that I had as a result. I worried not only about my own problems (which were plenty), but about my boss' as well. My non-existent boundaries at the time prevented me from setting limits with myself about what I would and would not allow. Even when my work started to suffer because of the stress I was under, and even when I felt so completely drained to the point that I would cry in the bathroom for hours at night, I couldn't tell my boss that I needed a break.

I thought that he wouldn't like me anymore if I wasn't there whenever he needed me. He knew that if he called at two in the morning and said he needed me to be in the office by five the next day I would be there. (And, yes, he actually did this! More than once.) I didn't want to disappoint him.

But once again, not setting boundaries and working too much lost me my job.

Hospitalized for Exhaustion

To make a long story short, I had a breakdown, and needed to be hospitalized.

You would think after everything I did for my boss, he would understand that I needed to rest for a week or so, and then let me come back to work. But they fired me because my boss said I couldn't handle the job's pressure. And, like I said, the emotional stress had make my work suffer. I had overdone it again.

Where Is the Middle Ground?

It's been almost two years since I've worked anywhere for a paycheck, and as much as I want—I need—a job, I'm terrified that I'll only fail again.

I suppose I still have to learn what my limitations as an employee are, and how to politely stand up for myself if those boundaries are crossed. It sounds so easy, doesn't it? If only it were.

Think About It

What is the biggest challenge you have faced when working with a coworker,

boss, or other authority figure? _____

_____

_____

_____

How did you handle it? _____

_____

_____

_____

Would you handle it any differently now? Why or why not? _____

_____

_____

_____

www.youthcomm.org

Work It Out at Work

June Deutsch, director of human resources at Project Hospitality in New York City, gives advice about how to handle a new job.

What kind of behavior is appropriate or inappropriate at work?

Answer: Of course there's basic politeness and respectfulness, not only normal good manners, but also respecting people's cultures, not using foul language, and the dirty joke thing—you don't want to make jokes that people might take the wrong way.

Other than that, professional environments can be very different. I've worked at a bank and at a social service agency, and there's huge differences between the two. They've got two totally separate sets of rules.

At a bank, everyone is dressed every day according to the dress code, it's rigid and it's about basic respect. Here at Project Hospitality, it is very touchy-feely. Because there's social workers and counselors, coworkers are much more attuned to people's feelings. If someone is crying, their coworker might sit down and ask, "What's going on?"

How can you handle a conflict with a boss or coworker?

Answer: If someone yells at you or pressures you to work hours you can't, sometimes you need to bite the bullet and talk to them, but do it in a nice way. Later on you should ask them to speak to you in private, never in front of other people. Be respectful even if they might not be.

Especially for a young person that's hard to do—to not be reactive to the situation. So stay calm and be forthright: "I'm really uncomfortable that you're snapping at me in front of other people." State the problem in a clear, concise way. Not nasty, not cursing. It's sometimes tough.

How can you figure out how to act at work?

Answer: If some people seem to come in late, or follow different rules, ask to speak to your supervisor in private and say, "I see some people do this and this, I just wonder if that applies to me." The manager should tell you what the rules are for you, and explain why the rules may not apply to others.

This is very important: You don't have to figure things out. You should come forward and ask. Make no assumptions, especially if you're brand new, because if you're wrong, you'll get in trouble. No one will fault you for asking a question, but they will if you act and it turns out you're wrong.

How can you handle a personal problem that interferes with work?

Answer: Be forthright. Go to your boss in a respectful way, in private. You don't have to explain the whole issue, but give a basic explanation, like, "My boyfriend and I split up and I'd like to take a day or two off." Just saying, "I have a personal problem" doesn't help out much. But be aware that they might not be able to give you what you ask for.

You have to work on your relationship with your manager. Asking questions and being respectful can give you the rapport where you can knock on the door if an issue comes up.

www.youthcomm.org

Quiet on the Job
I can't figure out how to act at work.

By DANIELLE WILSON

I get so mad and offended when teachers and coworkers say about me, "Danielle is a nice girl, but she's so quiet." I get fed up because I

Danielle Wilson

don't consider myself quiet at all. When they say that I am, it makes me feel frustrated and completely misunderstood.

But in a way I understand why they say that. You see, it's almost like there are two different Danielles inside of me. There is the At-Home-Danielle, who chills, laughs and jokes with her friends. And then there's the At-School-or-Work-Danielle who just goes to work or school to do what she gotta do and be out.

I worked as a receptionist in my school, where all I did was answer the phone and say, "Good afternoon, please hold." So there was no one to really talk to. But the truth is, if there was someone to talk to like a boss or secretary, I wouldn't say much anyway. That's because I don't feel I'd be able to talk to a boss or a coworker like I talk to my friends. I wouldn't know what to say.

Home vs. the Real World

I think everyone is a little different when they're at home than when they are in the real world. At home I live with my brother who is 20 and my sister who is 16. Between these two I feel like I'm the adult. I take care of my 16-year-old sister, pay the bills and go to school and work.

Even though my brother is older than I am, I've always been more responsible than he is. I sometimes have to tell him what to do, like, "Pick up your trash, Johnny!" "Wash the dishes, Johnny!" "Clean your room, Johnny!"

My aunt helps me with money, but she lives all the way across town so I don't see her that much.

Letting Loose With Friends

With my friends I let loose from all the responsibility. I bust out. Like one time, I was with my friend when this guy who had been stalking her knocked on the door. My friend didn't know how to tell him to leave her alone, but I did. I said, "Boy, you better listen and listen good. My friend Tiffany doesn't want you, never has and never will, so leave her alone, please, thank you kindly." Then I slammed the door in his face.

If my teachers or coworkers knew how I act at home, I don't think they'd believe it. They wouldn't say I was quiet at all.

Quiet on the Job

I think part of the reason I'm so different at home is because at home I don't have to answer to any adult or authority figure, except my aunt, "the big boss lady across town," and, well, she's all the way across town. So that means I can stay up as long as I want, have company any time I want, basically eat when I want and wherever I want. It also means I don't really know how to talk with authority figures. So at work or school I just stay quiet. I feel like if I remain quiet no one will notice that I'm there, then they can't tell me what to do.

> **I feel like if I remain quiet no one will notice that I'm there. Then they can't tell me what to do.**

But being quiet at work doesn't work all the time. It sometimes makes the boss pick on you more. When I was working at Pretzel Time, I had to give out samples of pretzels outside of the store to try to get customers to buy them. The other people who worked there would stand out with the samples while talking to people passing by and laughing with them. They would do practically anything to get those people to come in the store.

Criticized for Shyness

But I was quiet. All I would do is shout "Free samples!" I got a lot of greedy people taking the samples, but almost no one walking into the store. My boss criticized me for that.

And at an internship I had through my school, at a garden in a hospital, I also felt like being quiet made things harder for me. There was this other intern there from a college who would walk around with a pad and pencil and jot down every word our boss would say and ask like a million questions. My boss asked me, "Do you have any questions?" And I'd say, "No, I'm all right." But what I really wanted to say was, "The other intern already asked all I wanted to know. I don't think there's nothing left to ask."

Maybe I Need to Speak Up?

At the end of the internship, my boss told my teacher, "Oh, Danielle's a nice girl, but she's so quiet." I felt so misunderstood!

Then at my school, my mentor, who I think is mad cool, told me she was worried that I wouldn't do well on my final presentation for school because I'm quiet. I felt angry and hurt again.

But the truth is, if everyone is saying I'm quiet, maybe it is a problem that I feel so unlike myself when I'm at school or on the job.

I have this card that I picked up from a bookstore when I was about 10 or 11. It has pretty blue and pink clouds on it and on the top it has "DANIELLE" written in big, bold letters. After that it reads, "God is your only judge." I still have that card to this day. I know people will always have something to say about me whether it is good or bad. And it hurts to hear them say that I'm quiet at school and work when I know that's not my true self. Ultimately, that card is right—what they say doesn't matter and only God can judge me—and that card and my heart keep me grounded through all the criticism from bosses and teachers.

But I still hope that I can learn to feel more comfortable around authority figures. Maybe then they'll have a better idea of who the real me is, and it will be easier for me to be around them.

How to Keep Your Job

Once you have a job, you need to work hard to hold on to it. No matter what the job is—an internship, volunteer work, or a career job—show that you take it seriously. You can do this, and hold on to your job, if you:

1. Show Up on Time. Come to work every single day on time or earlier unless there's a real emergency, like you've been throwing up all night or you got into a car accident. If that happens, call at least an hour ahead of time to say you won't be in. (Always make sure to have your employer's phone number with you so you can do that.)

2. Follow Directions and Ask Questions. Do your best work, and ask questions when you aren't sure what is expected of you.

3. Get Along With Your Coworkers. Be respectful to those you work with and they will be more likely to act respectfully toward you. Don't curse people out. Avoid fights. Getting along with your boss and co-workers will bring you a long way.

Activity Page for Group Leaders

Acing a Job Interview

Topic: Acing a job interview

Goal: Help teens realize that a job interview (and the way they should behave on the job) is a little like acting. They have to learn to play the role, and they have to practice. Only when it starts to feel natural will the teens be able to perform well under the stress of a real job interview

Time: 5 minutes for each teen

■ **Tell teens:** When you meet someone for the first time on the job, you can't go wrong with the following:

1) Stand up (if you're sitting down).

2) Shake hands (firmly, but not like a vise grip).

3) While shaking hands, look the person in the eye.

4) Say: "Hi, I'm X. Thank you for interviewing me. I really appreciate the opportunity to talk with you."

(Teens can put this in their own words, but they need to do three things: state their name, thank the interviewer, and express their appreciation.)

Note: The "Making a Good Impression" exercise on p. 84 can supplement the lesson.

■ **Pick a teen to rehearse with you first.**

■ **Explain to other teens in group:** You are the "audience," and you need to look for four things. The teen should:

1) Stand up when the interviewer enters and approach him or her.

2) Reach out to initiate the handshake.

3) Look the interviewer in the eye while shaking hands.

4) Say the line above, or a reasonable variation on it.

■ **Explain to teens in group:** They need to give their peer constructive feedback on how well she does each of those things. (Remind them that they'll each get the chance to rehearse in a minute.)

■ **Bring teen to the front and have her sit down in a chair** (pretend it's a waiting area).

■ **Stand off to the side, and then walk in and call out the person's name.**

■ **Go through steps 1-4 above.**

■ **Before there are any comments, do it one more time with the same teen.**

■ **Ask group for a few quick constructive suggestions.**

■ **Repeat with the same teen two or three more times.** Asking the group for to give one piece of feedback each time (e.g., "maintain eye contact," or "grasp my hand a little more firmly").

■ **If you have time and a small enough group, repeat this with each member of the group,** in front of the group so that each student gets some direct feedback from you, and gets to "rehearse" their role in front of the "audience."

■ **Have the group practice on each other.** Tell them they must do the exercise 10 times each and they must give each other one piece of feedback each time.

<u>Closing discussion</u>: 5- 10 minutes

■ **Ask the teens what they learn.** Point out to the teens that a job interviewer is going to form an opinion of them in the first 30 seconds, and that getting off on the right foot can make the entire interview go much, much better.

My Job Interview

MAKING A GOOD IMPRESSION: *You are interviewing for a job. Check the boxes next to things you* <u>should do</u> *to get off to a good start in the job interview.*

☐ Shake the interviewer's hand before and after the interview

☐ Chew gum

☐ Answer my cell phone

☐ Look the interviewer in the eye

☐ Use slang

☐ Be early

☐ Show I'm interested in the job by asking questions about it

☐ Turn off the ringer on my cell phone

☐ Dress like I'm ready for a hot date

For answers see page 88.

ACING THE QUESTIONS: *Your interview is for the clothing store the GAP. The interviewer asks, "What will you bring to this job?" Circle any responses that apply to you. Then, give proof of it.*

EXAMPLE:

If you circle "I am responsible," you might write for your proof:

"I am responsible because I have looked after my baby sister after school for the last three years. My friends know me as the one who is always on time."

I am responsible.

Proof: _____

_____

_____

I am a hard-worker.

Proof: _____

_____

_____

I'll make a good sales person because I get along well with just about everyone.

Proof: _____

_____

_____

I am a team player.

Proof: _____

_____

_____

Now write two of your own:

I _____

Proof: _____

_____

_____

I _____

Proof: _____

_____

_____

The job interviewer will likely ask you, "What experience have you had?"

List all the experiences you have had that could help you at the job. Remember, even if you haven't had a paid job, chances are you have done other types of jobs that will show the interviewer you are responsible and a good worker, like taking care of a sibling, buying groceries for an elderly neighbor, tutoring younger kids at your school, babysitting, volunteering at church or playing on a team.

My experiences: _____

_____

_____

The job interviewer at the GAP (or any job) may well ask, "Why do you want this job?" Remember, you need to appeal to the interviewer here. So your response should be about what YOU can do for the GAP, not what the GAP can do for you. Check the boxes next to responses that you think would work:

☐ I like working with the public and I get along with just about everyone.

☐ I love fashion and I'm good at helping people pick out clothes they like.

☐ I love fashion and ultimately I want to have a career as a fashion designer.

☐ My friend who works here gets to buy your clothes and a discount and I want that discount too.

☐ I want the money.

For answers see page 88.

Now make up a few of your own for way you want the job: _____

_____

_____

www.youthcomm.org

Answers

For a job interview, I should:

☑ Shake the interviewer's hand before and after the interview

☐ Chew gum

☐ Answer my cell phone

☑ Look the interviewer in the eye

☐ Use slang

☑ Be early

☑ Show I'm interested in the job by asking questions about it

☑ Turn off the ringer on my cell phone

☐ Dress like I'm ready for a hot date

These are the appropriate answers to "Why do you want this job?"

☑ I like working with the public and I get along with just about everyone.

☑ I love fashion and I'm good at helping people pick out clothes they like.

☑ I love fashion and ultimately I want to have a career as a fashion designer.

☐ My friend who works here gets to buy your clothes and a discount and I want that discount too.

☐ I want the money.

www.youthcomm.org

Chapter 3
Your First Home After Care

Your First Home After Care: Why This Chapter Matters

I knew a girl named Shayne who was 18, living with her mother, and wanted so badly to have her own apartment.

She didn't have a job or a high school diploma. I asked her how she was going to support herself if she got her own place. She said, "Oh honey, that's why I have a man."

Tanya Soto

To make a long story short, things didn't work out as she had planned. She and her boyfriend fought all the time about how she didn't have a job. He threatened to move out and find someone else, and that's exactly what happened. Now she lives with her mom. (Big surprise.)

Shayne told me she should have waited to move out until she was ready, because now instead of saying, "That's why I have a man," she's saying, "That's why I have a mommy."

Almost all teens want to go out on their own. They want to get their own apartment or go to college (or maybe run away with Prince Charming).

Yet living on your own is serious. If you're not prepared for it, going out on your own can cause more harm than good.

There are questions you should ask yourself before making the decision to move out: Can you handle living alone? If you're moving in with a roommate, are both of you capable of working things out? Will you be able to pay bills on time?

I ask myself these questions because I'm in a group home, but in a year or so I will be moving into an independent living apartment. It's not exactly the same as being all on your own—you still have a social worker who will look out for you—but it's very different from what I'm used to.

I'm scared, because I wonder if I'll get along with my roommate. I'm scared, because after I leave this group home there won't be staff and residents to talk to and count on. But all these fears give me more motivation to do this.

This chapter focuses on living in your own home. Most teens in foster care eventually have to do it. Some of us are eager to live in our own apartments. Others are scared. Most of us are a little of both.

In the following stories, teens write about what it's like to live in a supervised independent living apartment (SILP) through their agency. They talk about some of the struggles, like battling loneliness. They also tell the joys—privacy, quiet, pride. We hope their stories help you prepare for the day you will step foot into the first home that's all yours.

—Tanya Soto

To Have Roommates or Not?

What I like most about being in my own place is that I don't have to worry about anybody being on my back about anything. When I was in my apartment the first few weeks I didn't have a roommate yet, and it was a little scary. When the time came for me to go to sleep the first night, I was so scared I had to sleep with the hallway light on. Since I got a roommate, things are different. I'm not scared at night now, but it was more comfortable when I was alone and had my privacy.

Angi

All to Myself

When I first moved into my own apartment, I sat in the middle of my floor and cried and thought, 'This is it?' Then I thought, 'This is mine. So long as I pay rent, no one can take it away from me.' And that's the first time I felt like something was really mine. I was happy and absolutely terrified. I'm still terrified I'm not going to make it.

Christine McKenna

On Our Own

Apartment programs let teens try out living on their own *before* they leave care.

By TABITHA KOZAKIEWICZ

Barbara Moore, a 19-year-old New York City chick, lives it up in her own apartment in Harlem, which she shares with a roommate. Last time

Tabitha Kozakiewicz

I visited, Barbara and her roommate were just chillin', eating KFC, and Barbara was rocking tight striped pants and braids. She was talking about what it was like to live in her own apartment for the first time.

Her apartment is hooked up real nice. She has cable, a phone she shares with her roommate, and rapper pics all over her bedroom. The apartment has shiny hardwood floors, big rooms and freshly painted walls.

Barbara's life isn't bad either. She has a job working with 4th grade kids and she is also attending a college where she can get both her G.E.D. and a degree the same time—holla! Basically Barbara's trying to do her thing. She's only 19 but is becoming an independent woman.

But did you know she is one of us? I mean, Barabara is in foster care. She is part of a housing program called SILP, which stands for Supervised Independent Living Program.

Real Apartments, Real Life Experience

SILP is a national program, but sometimes it has different names in different agencies and states. It is designed to help prepare teens in care to live on their own by putting them in their own apartments.

By living on their own with a roommate, teens in SILP apartments learn important skills before they age out of care, like how to cook meals (or pick up KFC), do their own laundry, and shopping, and get along with their neighbors. If they need help or run into trouble, because they're still in foster care a social worker will come to their rescue.

www.youthcomm.org

The Support of a Social Worker

There are often conditions for living in a SLIP, such as being 18, and having a job or attending school. Teens often share their SILP apartment with another person in the program. They get to meet their roommate ahead of time, to see if they basically get along.

A social worker checks up on them in their apartment from time to time, and they still attend independent living classes. There are general rules teens in SILP must follow, like they still have a curfew and they can't have family, friends, or a boyfriend or girlfriend live in the apartment. If they can't really manage the responsibilities of living alone—like if they go wild and have too many loud parties and the landlord complains (that happened to Barbara once)—they can be sent back to a group home or foster home.

The SILP program began when people realized that independent living classes alone can't truly prepare teens to live on their own. It's hard to learn skills like cooking or shopping in a classroom. So someone got the bright idea to put teens in their own apartments, where they would get actual experience living on their own. If they needed help, their social worker could lend a hand.

But there aren't a lot of SILP apartments, so not everyone in foster care gets to do it. Being in SILP is a privilege, said Raqueil Shelton, Barbara's social worker. Shelton said they pick the teens they can trust the most to live alone without getting in trouble.

Barbara was one of those teens who proved herself responsible. She changed a lot during her last few years in group homes and foster homes. She stopped partying as much, she was going to school regularly, and in the group home she kept to herself instead of getting into all the drama. So Shelton let Barbara join SILP.

Drive-by Supervision?

Barbara's glad. She really likes living in her own apartment and plans to stay there until she ages out of foster care.

The best thing about living in SILP, Barbara said, is that she gets to be herself—she can come home and relax and eat when she wants to. She also gets privacy, which is hard to come by in a foster or group home. She feels good knowing that if something goes wrong, like if she doesn't follow the rules, she doesn't become homeless. She will just go back to a foster home.

But it's not all easy. She got in trouble with the landlord once because her friends were smoking in the hallway and being loud. Also, she sometimes has trouble paying the phone bill, and finds herself feeling lonely from time to time.

Not everyone agrees it is a good idea to put teens in care in their own apartments. Some people say the program gives teens a false idea of what it means to be independent. After all, in a SILP apartment your rent is paid for and you receive money for food. That doesn't happen when you're truly on your own.

> **The best thing about living in a housing program, Barbara said, is that she gets to be herself—she can come home and relax and eat when she wants to.**

For the most part, the teens I talked to who did SILP found it useful. Before he left care, Lenny Jones lived in an apartment like Barbara's, with a roommate from his agency. Like with Barbara, the other people in Lenny's building were not in foster care. Lenny and his roommate had to cook and do everything for themselves. "In the group home you never wanted to learn how they made that nasty food, so I definitely didn't learn how to cook it there," said Lenny.

For the most part, Lenny liked living in SILP. His only problem was adjusting to his first roommate, who was very different from him.

'Get Help While You Can'

But even with experience living in a SILP apartment, when Lenny first left care, he struggled. He had to sleep on a friend's couch for months when he decided to leave his college dorm. Eventually he found an apartment, which he shares with a roommate. Lenny said that it's good to live on your own, but it's also good to have a roommate there too. Not only does it cut the rent in half, said Lenny, but "there is always people there to chill with. And in case you slip in the tub, fall on the floor and

www.youthcomm.org

die, someone will open the door and find your body." He's joking, I hope.

Princess Carr had her share of troubles, too. Though she lived in a transitional apartment where she learned a lot of independent living skills, she eventually ran away from it. And after leaving foster care, she was homeless for a while.

"When you're a teenager and you're going through growing pains and you're in a good situation," said Princess, "you still always think you could do better. You always think that whatever situation you're in that they're not treating you right. You think, 'I'm grown. I should get this. I should get that.' And you don't see it for what it really is: help."

Princess' advice to teens preparing to live on their own is to accept help when it's offered. That's what teens living in SILP apartments are trying to do. Hopefully, it'll teach them how to better help themselves when they're out on their own.

My Own Two Feet

An independent living program helped me get running.

By SCOTT BURKE

When I first came to my group home, staff told me that kids who do well go to an independent living program called 112. At 112, you buy and cook your own food, buy and wash your own clothes with your own money, take care of your own medical appointments and so on. The benefit is that you can go out whenever you want and stay out until curfew, which is at 10:30.

Scott Burke

In group homes you don't have to take care of so many chores, but you have to deal with a lot of rules. Independent living programs are just the opposite. You have to take care of yourself and your mess, but you do have a lot of freedom. So automatically I wanted to go there.

When I was almost 18, staff asked what I planned to do until I'm 21. I said I wanted to go to 112. It sounded like a good way to prepare to live by myself. Staff took me to court where they told me I could move to 112. I was so happy.

Heavy Bags in the Heat

Then I had to apply for Supplemental Security Income (SSI), because at 112 you need SSI to help you pay the rent. To get SSI you have to have a disability. I don't know what my disability is. To me, I don't even have a disability. So I can't say I am too proud or happy about getting SSI, but it pays the bills. I get $634 each month.

Finally the day I was to move hit and I was out. But I was in for a long, tiring day. First they messed up my allowance so I didn't have money to get a cab to take my stuff over there. I had to carry all of my heavy bags over there one by one, while the heat was at its highest.

It took me nine trips back and forth until I was done. When I finally finished moving I was exhausted, but I thought it was all worth it.

Hot Pockets for Dinner

I got lucky and got the room on the third floor that I wanted. (It had a cable wire so I get cable in my room for free.) My room is small but I'm not complaining. I have a dresser and a bed with some drawers in the bottom. I have a TV sitting on a chair, two tanks holding lizards and a window.

After I set up my room, I noticed I was without food, money and supplies. So I got my allowance and went to the supermarket to get my first load of groceries: ham and cheese, mayonnaise, bread, some Hot Pockets, chicken nuggets, soda, juice, laundry detergent and cereal.

I carried everything home and put it in my own cabinet and my spot in the fridge, which I share with four people. Then I microwaved some Hot Pockets and drank soda. (I know how to cook Italian, but for now I'm sticking with TV dinners, those joints you put in the freezer and just heat up.)

I still wasn't done with my chores, though. I had to go get a new laundry cart because the one they had was broken. Then I took my clothes to the laundromat and washed them.

On My Own. . .Sort Of

By the end, I was a little tired of doing all this, but I also felt like it was preparing me for adulthood so I didn't mind. It felt good to choose what I was going to eat and when I was going to do my laundry. I sort of enjoyed doing all that hard work.

When I was done I went for a long walk with a good friend who moved in at the same time as me. We walked for a good hour and caught some numbers from some shorties, then headed back.

When we got back, I made a sandwich, washed out my dishes and went to my room. I watched cable TV for a while and then went down to the stoop of the building to smoke a cigarette and chill. Part of me felt like I was on my own, but in a funny way, I also felt just the same.

Learning to Budget

On my second day, staff warned us not to do anything stupid, like bring in drugs or alcohol or come home under the influence. If we did that, we could be kicked out. For those of us who are too old to return to foster care and have no place to go, that means a homeless shelter.

They also explained that we'd get our SSI in an allowance of about $100 each week. It feels good having my own money and being able to buy what I want and need. But it's good that they don't give us the entire $634 at once, 'cause I might spend it too fast.

Still, I am learning to budget my money. On Friday, when I get my check, I put all of it in the bank except for $20 to $40 to spend on myself. On Monday I get about $40 to spend on groceries and $10 to $20 for pocket change. Wednesday I get most of the rest for pocket money, and then everything repeats itself. I've also been looking for a job so that I can save more money for an apartment on my own.

> **I like that I am completely responsible for everything that goes on in my life.**

Choosing My Own Path

I'm a lot happier now that I can actually live a life. In my group home, my day was over at 6 p.m. Now, my day just gets started at that time. I have more time to chill with my peoples.

The IL program is also better than a group home because most of the kids there are all cool, getting by on their own. I like that I am completely responsible for everything that goes on in my life. I would have it no other way.

Crib Sheet
How to find your own place.

By SCOTT BURKE

Scott Burke

I know some of you are eager to leave foster care, but don't rush it. Before you leave care, make sure you have a place to stay—and not just for a few nights. Living in foster care is a whole lot better than living in the streets or in Covenant House, or just kicking around from place to place. That makes it hard to get or keep a job, or to continue school.

When you are about two years away from emancipating from care, it's time to start thinking about how to find an apartment, where to look or what to look for. Here are some steps that can make looking for an apartment a little easier.

1. Plan Ahead. Find out from your social worker (or whoever in your agency can tell you) what benefits you can get when you leave foster care (like a housing voucher, income through SSI or special housing for former foster youth). Find out how old you have to be to receive these benefits. Get as much information as you can about options for when you leave care.

Start figuring things out early, said Harriet Cohen of Schaffer Hall. Even though some foster youth are eligible for housing vouchers, it's not a simple process to get the voucher and find a place. "Timing is one of the big things that can go wrong in an apartment search," Cohen said. "People don't apply for the housing voucher in time. It takes six months to a year to have it secure."

2. Know Your Options. One thing you're going to need to do is figure out where you want to live and what kind of apartment you want. You may want to live in your own studio apartment, or you might want to live with roommates. You might be planning to fall back on relatives. Find out now if that's realistic.

If you decide you want your own place, think about exactly what you're looking for in an apartment. Some people want to live in a quiet place, others want to be close to friends or family.

3. Save Money. You need a bank account with savings in it. When you finally do move into your apartment, you're not only going to need your first month's rent, you're also going to need a security deposit. That's money the landlord takes from you and holds onto in case you mess up the apartment in any way or leave without paying some of your rent. When you move out, the landlord should give it back to you...unless you screw up. Sometimes landlords want a security deposit and the last month's rent, in advance. You need to be prepared.

4. Get References. Your landlord will need references—people he can talk to about how you'll be as a tenant. Basically, the landlord wants to know if you'll pay the rent on time and be a nice neighbor, that you won't have loud parties or disrespect the apartment. So you should ask someone—like a teacher, a staff member, job supervisors or any adult that has been in your life—if you can use them as a reference. Make sure you have that person's number to give to the landlord so he or she can call.

5. Start Searching. Six or seven months before you're ready to leave the system is a good time to start looking for an apartment. To find a place, go to neighborhoods you want to live in and look for signs, and put up your own signs. (That's especially good if you're looking for a roommate.) Look in newspapers or online, like on Craig's List if your town has one, and ask your agency about real estate agents, even though brokers can get expensive. And ask everyone you know if they know of a place for rent.

Look for things like location. Is it close to the bus or train, your job or school, or a grocery store? If sunlight is important to you, look for a place that has a nice angle toward the sun. But you're not going to get all of these things so your best bet is to narrow down your priorities and look for what you need, not what you want. I would look for how close it is to work, the store and the post office.

6. Dress for Success. When meeting with a broker or apartment manager, act as if you're going on a job interview. Put on your most professional clothes, use your best speaking voice, be on time and have a positive attitude. Fill out apartment applications neatly. Have your ID and other information handy.

www.youthcomm.org

7. Ask Questions.
Ask about anything you're unsure of or don't understand. For example, some places include heat and hot water in the rent, some don't. It can get pretty expensive to pay for those things, so make sure you ask whether they're included. If there's anything wrong with the apartment—like the lights or windows are broken—make sure they'll be repaired before you move in. Also, if you're moving to an unfamiliar neighborhood, ask people around there if it's safe, and try walking around after dark to see how you feel. You may want to bring someone with you to see the apartments or meet with a landlord, so you remember to ask your questions and have help thinking through your choices.

8. Read the Lease.
Leases are not easy to understand. They're usually many pages long and have a lot of sections and clauses. Read the whole thing and make sure you understand all the rules before you sign it. Never sign anything unless you absolutely understand and agree to the terms.

If the lease says 'no pets' and you get a cat, you can get kicked out. The best idea is to show the lease to an adult you trust—before you sign it. Once you sign the lease, you can't get your money back. So be careful.

9. Keep it Down.
When the time comes for throwing yourself a housewarming party, invite your neighbors and landlord if it's appropriate. Don't let your guests disturb other tenants in the building, and be sure to end the party at a reasonable hour. Enjoy your freedom, but remember—you can be kicked out for disturbing your neighbors.

Apartment Hunting?

Terms you should know.

Efficiency: a one-room apartment with its own bathroom, but not necessarily a complete kitchen. You might share a kitchen with others.

Studio: a one-room apartment with its own kitchen and bathroom. Basically you live and sleep in one room.

Broker's fee: The amount of money you pay an apartment broker or realtor for finding you an apartment. Remember: If you don't use a broker, you don't pay a broker's fee. Read apartment notices on telephone poles. Ask friends for tips. Try to avoid that broker's fee!

Credit check fee: The landlord may check your credit rating and charge you a credit check fee of about $25. (This is a routine check into your financial status, and does not indicate whether you were in foster care.)

First month's rent: Just that—the first month's rent you pay the landlord when you move in.

Security deposit: This is usually equal to one month's rent, but some landlords require more. The deposit money is returned to you after you move out, unless the landlord keeps the deposit to pay for unpaid rent or damage to the apartment.

Lease: A written contract that the tenant (you) and landlord sign, requiring the tenant to live in an apartment for a specific period of time (usually one to three years) for a set amount of rent.

—Joanne Sala

www.youthcomm.org

Other than renting my own apartment, what options do I have for housing?

College dorm/off/campus housing:
You can go away to college and live in a dorm or in an off-campus apartment, which can be a lot cheaper than the city. Also, many colleges have bulletin boards or housing offices that list apartments for rent or people looking for roommates.

Sharing an apartment:
Consider sharing an apartment with a friend. If you don't know of anyone who is interested in sharing an apartment, you can go to a roommate service, which will charge a fee for finding you a roommate, or you can look at the apartment listings at the college office, or on Craig's List or other online services.

SRO's:
SRO's (that stands for Single Room Occupancy) are buildings or hotels where you can rent a single room. Landlords usually try to rent out these rooms on a daily basis at a high daily rent, but in some cities there is a way to become a "rent stabilized" tenant in an SRO at a reasonable weekly rate.

Getting Back to You

Part of independent living is dealing with yourself.

By XAVIER REYES

I remember when it was almost my turn to leave the system I had come to know and love. I was excited, grateful and joyful. Ah, to be

Xavier Reyes

free of the social workers who hounded me, the staff who controlled me, and the peers who annoyed me! What more could I ask for?

The thing I knew I'd miss (and I do), is the free food and rent. So, a few months before I aged out, I did my best to make sure that I would be ready to provide for myself. I had an apartment ready and a job to pay for it.

But while I had taken care of everything on the outside, things were different on the inside of me.

Mostly, I started to realize I had become dependent on the very system I was sick of. I wasn't just financially dependent on the foster care system, I was also emotionally dependent. Yes! Emotionally!

In the system, any time I had a problem, I could count on my social worker or staff or other residents to talk to about it. Who would I talk to when I was on my own? I knew that if I was going to make it, I needed to learn how to help myself and check in with me instead of me checking in with someone else—not just for the practical stuff, but for the emotional things, too. I needed to set my own goals and deal with my own issues.

Get to Know Yourself

Some people never learn how to deal with themselves and the difficult parts of their lives, and that can hurt them later on. I know a few people who used to live in foster care who never learned to hold down a job, partly because they let their personal problems interfere with their work. Now they rely on welfare. I also know people who have so much anger that they can't form healthy relationships. All the time they were in the system, they were angry at other people for holding them back. But now the main thing holding them back is their own anger.

One important lesson I learned is that part of learning to live independently is being able to put some closure on that experience called foster care. It's over now, and I have to put it behind me. People who don't do that use the system as an excuse. You'll hear them say, "The system made me this way," or, "If I had lived at home, things would be different today."

> **We may have learned how to cook and balance a checkbook, but we haven't learned how to be alone.**

But how do you put closure on such a big and difficult experience in your life, such as being in foster care? For me, I had to allow myself to reflect on all that I'd been through and feel the emotions of it all.

I had to let go of the anger, the pain, and the blame as much as I could. As I did that, it was easier to move on and look for things that I'd learned from the experience. And it's easier to avoid making the same mistakes or getting into the same difficult situations.

In order to do that, you may need to take time to focus on yourself.

Thoughts of My Past

Before I left the system, I spent a lot of time alone in the Supervised Independent Living Program. I lived in an apartment by myself for a few months. I used this time alone to work on some of my problems and to set goals for myself.

My apartment was located by Riverside Park in New York City. Several times during the week, I would wake up really early and go walking along the river. When I first started walking, I really didn't think about much. I was too caught up in the views—watching the sunrise over the city. But eventually, thoughts of my past just flowed through me.

I was able to step back and review what had happened in my life. Some of what I remembered was painful. I remembered being abused when I was younger and I remembered the day I knew that my drug use had become excessive. I recalled how I felt at those moments, and accepted responsibility for my part in all that had happened.

Eventually I started thinking about the future. I thought about the goals I wanted to achieve. I wanted, one day, to move to Florida, and buy a home. I knew that to get that I needed an education and a well-paying job, so I decided to go back to school. When I aged out, I was going to be crossing a major bridge in my life and I wanted to be ready for it.

It Pays Off Tenfold

After my walks, I'd feel full of energy, like I was ready to take on anything. I'd feel relieved and rejuvenated, like a football team after a power session with the coach.

I still remember those walks. Taking that time out to face my emotions and figure out my goals has paid off. I have a sense of direction in my life, and I've been following many of the plans that I first made while walking along Riverside Park.

I now work as the director of administration for a community foundation. I went back to school and completed two semesters of college. I still want to move to Florida and buy a house, and I want to adopt a kid when I get older.

Leaving care wasn't easy for me. But taking the last year to get to know myself and figure out what I wanted from life helped to make it smoother.

Facing the Future Strong

So I urge everyone who is getting close to aging out to get a job, save money, and learn to cook...but also don't forget to take time out for yourself, too. Take time to plan your future and think about your dreams. Take time to reflect on the things you have experienced and how they have affected you. It can be scary, but don't let that stop you.

Do a self-assessment of your needs: What have you learned from your experience in foster care? How have you grown? What areas in your life do you need to work on? What are your goals and how are you going to achieve them?

It's so easy for us to lose our sense of self after spending time in a system where we have to deal with so many different personalities on

a daily basis. In care, we can spend most of our time reacting to other people's rules and moods. But when we're on our own, we have to take action. We have to make decisions for ourselves.

Being able to live independently means being able to think independently, and to think independently you have to take time out for you. Turn off the TV and the phone. Put down the blunt and the beer. Go for a walk by yourself. Pick up a pen and your journal if that suits you. Look hard at yourself, where you come from, where you want to go, and what you need to get there. Getting back to you will help give you a clearer vision of where you are going and where you have been.

As Shakespeare wrote in Hamlet, "Know thyself and to thy own self be true." Being independent is more than what you do for yourself on the outside; it is also what you do for yourself on the inside.

Activity Page for Group Leaders

Finding and Keeping a Home

Topic: How to find and keep an apartment.

Goal: To help teens understand what they need to do to find an apartment.

Time: 1 hour

What you'll need: pencils, 3x5 cards or sheets of paper, flip chart or blackboard.

Warm-up activity: 10 minutes

■ **Freewrite:** Read the following prompts out loud and give teens 2 minutes to respond. Tell teens that grammar and spelling don't count. The important thing is to get their ideas on paper. The only rule is that they have to keep their pencils moving, even if they're writing "I don't know what to write."

"Describe the ideal home where you would live after care. For instance, what would it look like? How would it be furnished? Where would it be located—close to school, your job, or your family? Who would you live with, if anyone? How would it feel to be in your home?"

Note: Teens working independently can fill ou the worksheet on p. 112.

■ **Discuss freewrite (optional):** Ask for volunteers to read their freewrite.

Lesson: 50 minutes

■ **Set up the activity:** Divide your class into teams. Tell the students that Scott Burke, the writer, is 19 and has lived everywhere from psychiatric lockdowns to an independent living apartment. He knows what it takes to get and keep an apartment, and in this story he shares his hard-earned knowledge.

■ **Read and make lists:** Scott's "crib sheet" story on page 100 is divided into nine sections. In most of the sections, he gives several pieces of advice. Assign each team to read one or more sections and list his suggestions. Many youth may have trouble picking out the specific suggestions. As they're working on this, walk around the room and give them suggestions. (Answers to this are on p. 111).

■ **Discuss for 30 minutes:** On the board or flip chart write the first heading, "Plan Ahead." Ask the team that had that section to give their list of Scott's suggestions. Write them on the flip chart. If they've

Activity Page for Group Leaders

(continued)

missed some, ask if they'd like to include them. (It's OK for the teens to debate whether something should be included, and it's OK not to include everything.)

When the list is done, ask the teens if they agree with Scott: Are these things that people should do? Would they add anything? Which item do they think is most important? Are any of the items too hard or unrealistic?

Proceed through the story, putting each heading on the flip chart, getting the list from the teens, and discussing or debating the items on the list. Remember: Your goal is not to get a complete list or to have the teens give the "right" answers. You just want to spark a discussion.

For example, when you cover the "get references" section, you might go around the room and ask each teen to name one person they could use as a reference. This gets them thinking about who their potential resources are, and also lets them know that it's important to have those people in their lives.

At the end, ask whether they think Scott likes to play his music loud or act rowdy (he does). So why does he say you shouldn't do that in your first apartment? (Scott has learned to curb some of his desires for his own long-term good.)

By the time you're done, the teens themselves will have raised and discussed a lot of the main issues involved in getting an apartment. **Note:** Scott made his own list (p. 111). Tell teens to turn to p. 111 or copy that page and hand out to teens. Tell them to add anything he has left out.

■ **Freewrite:** Tell teens to freewrite to the following prompt: "Thinking about an apartment, what makes you anxious? Does Scott offer any helpful suggestions about what you can do to feel less anxious? If not, what do you think you can do?" **(Discuss this freewrite if you have time.)**

Scott's Crib Sheet for Finding and Keeping an Apartment

1. Find Out What Benefits You Can Get

- Find out how old you have to be to get benefits

- Get information about other options

- Apply 6 months ahead of time for housing vouchers

2. Know Your Options

- Where do you want to live?

- What kind of apartment do you want?

- Do you want a roommate?

- Are there relatives you could live with?

- Make a list of your priorities

3. Save Money

- Open a bank account

- Start saving money

- Save enough money to move into an apartment, including last month's rent and damage deposit

4. Get References

- Ask someone if you can use them as a reference

- List several people who you could use as references with their contact info

5. Start Searching

- Start looking 6-7 months before you leave

- Look in newspapers and online

- Ask your agency

- Ask everyone you know

6. Dress for Success

- Wear professional clothes

- Use your best speaking voice

- Be on time

- Have a positive attitude

- Have ID and other information handy

7. Ask Questions

- Does the rent include heat and hot water?

- Is there anything in the apartment that should be repaired?

- Does the neighborhood feel safe?

- Do you want to bring someone with you to look at the apartment?

8. Read the Lease

- Find an adult you trust to read the lease and explain it to you

- Pay special attention to things that concern you, such as a ban on pets

9. Keep It Down

- Don't blast your music.

My First Apartment

PLAN AHEAD: *Ask your social worker or independent living coordinator about resources or money you'll get when you leave care.*

What benefits will you get when you leave foster care? These can include discharge grants and housing vouchers.

1._____   4._____

2._____   5._____

3._____   6._____

For each benefit, when do you need to apply?

1._____   4._____

2._____   5._____

3._____   6._____

KNOW YOUR OPTIONS:

Where do you want to live—close to school, your job, or your family? Why?

_____

_____

What would be your ideal living situation? How would your apartment be furnished? _____

_____

_____

Do you want a roommate to save money? Why or why not? _____

_____

_____

Are there relatives you could live with? If so, who? _____

_____

_____

SAVE MONEY:

Have you opened a bank account and started to save money for your apartment including last month's rent and deposit? If not, why not? If so, good for you! How much money have you saved?

_____

_____

GET REFERENCES:

Who can you use as a reference for renting an apartment? (List all the people—social workers, teachers, employers, or other adults in your life who will put in a good word for you and any contact info you have for them.)

_____

_____

_____

START SEARCHING:

What newspapers or online sites can you look for to find an apartment?

1._____   4._____

2._____   5._____

3._____   6._____

Who in your agency can you ask for help? _____

_____

_____

Who else could help you find an apartment? _____

_____

_____

ALWAYS VIEW THE APARTMENT BEFORE RENTING:

What will you wear? (Dress for success!) _____

_____

_____

What questions will you ask? (For instance, "Are heat and hot water

included in the rent?") _____

_____

_____

SIGN THE LEASE:

What adult do you trust to read the lease and explain it to you?

_____

_____

_____

Chapter 4

Building Your
Support System

Building Your
Support System:
Why This Chapter Matters

When we think of life after foster care, we often think about the practical skills we need to make it, like cooking or finding a job. We sometimes forget about the emotional skills we need.

Most of us have been through a lot of hard times. For starters, we've all had to learn how to live apart from our families. And while we like to think that our life starts over when we leave care—and in many ways it does—the truth is that our painful experiences come with us. If we don't learn how to deal with our emotions, they can make it hard for us to work through problems at a job, deal with difficult landlords, and find people to support us when we feel lonely or sad.

Working through that emotional stuff isn't easy, and it takes time. So be patient with yourself.

But it is a good idea to begin thinking about it as soon as you feel ready. To help you do that, this chapter focuses on the emotional side of aging out. All the baggage that follows you even after you leave care can make you stronger and wiser in the end, but in the short term can cause you some chaos.

Who Can I Count On?

Leaving foster care has its ups and downs. The up part of it was being out of the system, doing your own thing. The down part was just being scared about what happens if you fall on your ass. What if you lose your job or get evicted from your apartment? On the one hand you want to be responsible, on the other hand you're worried about what will happen if things fall apart.

Lenny Jones

Running Scared

My first year out of foster care I was on the streets. I was homeless and I had nowhere to run. It was horrible. When I was in foster care, if I ran away or I ended up in the hospital, somebody from the agency would pick me up. When I aged out and I was on the streets, there was nobody coming around the corner saying, 'Princess, come on, let's go home.' I still felt like I needed someone to come and hold my hand and tell me, 'It's going to be all right.'

Princess Carr

www.youthcomm.org

Phoenix Rising

I made it, but I needed all the help I could get.

By CHRISTINA McKENNA

When I was getting ready to emancipate from foster care on my 18th birthday, I couldn't wait to be free, to spread my wings and fly. When

Christine McKenna

I thought of life after care, I imagined a beautiful two-bedroom apartment, a cat, a wonderful day job, school in the evenings, parties and dates galore. I would always have money to spend.

In other words, I had no clue what was in store for me.

I sometimes compare my emancipation from Los Angeles' foster care system to the release of a bird who's been kept in a cage for too many years. Once released a bird is bound to do one of two things: stay in the cage even though the door is now open, terrified of the world they're supposed to enter, or fly around chaotically, never knowing where to nest, where to call home. I took both routes.

How Much Toilet Paper Lasts a Month?

At first I tried to do the responsible thing, I really did. I got myself into a program at the YWCA, where I lived with six other females who had all recently left care. We roomed in a huge house, kind of like a college dorm. Then I sort of lied on a resume—don't try this at home, kids—to get a part time job as a secretary at a law firm. I also started going to college full time. I convinced myself that I was fine, that I could do this independent thing, it was no big deal. But I also knew that I had no idea what I was doing.

No one had ever sat down and taught me how to balance a checkbook, how to handle college (which, contrary to popular belief, is nothing like high school!) I had no idea how much toilet paper could last a month. Things like that were always just there in the group home. I never wondered how they got there. And I didn't even know how to socialize with people who hadn't also been in foster care.

Growing up, the only kids I got to hang out with had had as difficult lives as I had. I didn't know how to interact with people who thought it was weird to run screaming up and down the halls just because you were bored.

I Moved 3,000 Miles

I started to doubt whether I could survive this independence. This emancipation. I now understood why some slaves kept working for their masters even after they were freed. They had been given no more to cope in the real world than I had when I left care.

Eventually it occurred to me that maybe I would do better living farther away from my family. I imagined that they were just waiting for me to fail, and I was determined to prove them wrong. The problem was, I really was struggling, and I didn't want them to see that. I wanted to struggle my way to success somewhere far away from them, where they wouldn't see the times I stumbled. So I made the quick decision to move to New York. I had always wanted to live there.

This is the part where the bird who's been let out of his cage starts to fly all willy-nilly with no sense of direction.

Now mind you, I told nobody about my decision to move because I knew they would talk me out of it, because this was a stupid and impulsive plan. I was determined to do this on my own, with no help from anyone, even if it meant falling flat on my face in a pond of quicksand. I thought the only way to be truly independent was to never ask for help. Damn my stupid 18-year-old way of thinking!

> **I thought the only way to be truly independent was to never ask for help. Damn my stupid 18-year-old way of thinking!**

So I arrived off the bus in a New York City summer with nowhere to stay and no money. I kept telling myself, "It's all going to work out."

I Would Not Ask for Help

How and why it was going to work out I didn't let myself think about. Instead, I felt suddenly tempted to call my mentor, Pamela, back

www.youthcomm.org

in California, to bail me out of yet another jam. But then I decided that I was an adult now, and I had gotten myself into this, and I would not ask for help.

In the end though, I did accept help, but from a stranger instead of someone I knew. A lady saw me crying and when I told her why I was upset, she did the sweetest thing. She got me a room for the night at the Y.

The next day a police officer told me about a shelter called Covenant House, which was for kids under 21. Now I know it sounds ridiculous, but I still had that pride thing going on and I was completely against the idea of going to a shelter. In my twisted way of thinking, going to a shelter seemed another way of failing to be independent. I hadn't traveled over 3,000 miles to just end up back in a state's care!

Or perhaps I had, because that's exactly what happened.

Stuck at the Homeless Shelter

I entered Covenant House three days after I arrived in New York. I was struck with how similar this place was to my previous group homes. I was sleeping on a floor with close to 60 females, and we had to be in bed by 9:30. Once again I was dependent on others to take care of me, and it made me upset.

At Covenant House they put me in their psychiatric day treatment center because in foster care I had been diagnosed with many psychiatric illnesses. That meant I was not allowed to work. Instead, they wanted me and all the other "patients" in the program to sit on our fat asses and collect SSI money from the government, which is basically welfare for the mentally ill.

I Wanted Out

Ooooh, I was so mad. I wanted to work! I wanted to be a productive member of society!! I wanted to be independent! So I secretly began working at a not-for-profit organization. I became really close to my bosses, Tim and Jason, in the few months I worked there. I was like the lost little child they could help, and I needed their help badly. Accepting their support and company and encouragement and even, at times, money was when I began to believe that people could help me without taking away my sense of independence. Becoming independent, I began to see, was a long, slow, gradual process, and I needed all the help I could get. But I still couldn't wait to get there.

Before long, I wanted to move out of Covenant House. I wanted to try being on my own again. So I found a room for rent. The room cost way more than I could afford but I just had to have it. I wanted to move on.

Everyone, including Tim and Jason and the staff at Covenant House, tried to talk me out of it. It was amazing. I had all these people I had only known for less than three months trying to save me from myself just because they cared. But in my severe state of not-thinkingness, I was sure that the only reason everyone wanted me to not move was because nobody really wanted me to be independent. So I moved.

Scraping for Rent Money

I regretted it almost immediately. There was no way my part time job could pay for this $400 a month room which was more like a walk-in closet. Thank God I had friends—Tim and Jason—who each paid for a month's rent. I was nearing my second month in this hell of a place and once again becoming antsy and claustrophobic and running out of friends when another good person offered me help.

> **Becoming independent, I began to see, was a long, slow, gradual process, and I needed all the help I could get.**

A worker from Covenant House who I kept in contact with off and on told me that the check from the government I never wanted but would now kill to get my hands on finally came through, and there was an opening at a residential treatment program for mentally ill adults where I could have my own studio apartment. Normally I would have frowned at this—you know me, doing so well at the self-sufficient thing—but strike me dead if I didn't want to hop right through the phone and plant a big wet one right on her!

Supervised Housing Program, My Savior!

So I moved into the program. In some ways it was a lot like being in foster care all over again. Staff kept an eye on me. There was a lot of drama among the residents.

Still, I had my own apartment, I paid rent, well, sort of, and I had no curfew. It was a good combination of being independent and supported. I figured that if I didn't take it as an opportunity to get my crap together here, I would always be running and falling flat on my face.

I was only allowed to stay in the program for three years. When I was coming up on my second year there, I knew it was time to start planning for my future. So I started the process of applying a government program that allows people with low incomes—that's me—to find apartments they can afford.

While I waited to see if I would get approved for it, I tried not to not think too much about living completely on my own. If I did, I'd panic. So I decided to do this one step at a time, never thinking about more than what I was doing in a particular step. That kept me calmer.

> **When you're in care, you think that leaving care is going to make all your problems go away. What you don't realize is how you'll have a whole set of new ones.**

I Found an Apartment

After I received my voucher I went through the apartment hunting ritual still trying not to think. I found a really nice studio in the Bronx (OK, so what if a matchbox would've looked great to me!) and immediately started the process of making this apartment my home, which had a lot of steps to it. Somewhere between having the apartment approved by a worker and picking up the paperwork that would let me move in, the realization that this was it hit me so hard that I was paralyzed with fear.

Suddenly I wasn't so sure I could do it. I mean, I had already emancipated once in California and look how well that had turned out for me! Suddenly I wanted nothing more than to make it stop. I wanted to stay where I was safe, at the residential treatment home for mentally ill adults. I wasn't ready for the world outside that bubble I lived in.

But Could I Make It?

My therapist was the one who pretty much snapped me out of it. She said that I had basically two choices: I could either stay dependent on others to take care of me but still complain about how nobody treated me like an adult, or I could gather up my courage, face my fear, and just do it. I would never know what I was capable of doing until I tried.

She reminded me that I had already survived so much in my 21 years on this earth, more than most people do in their entire lives, and that I could get through this.

She was right. I could do this. It might be scary and paralyzing and everything else I feared it would be, but it would also be awesome! I love new adventures, and I realized this was just one of a million more I would have to go through in my life.

One Year Later...

Well, it's been over a year since I moved into that apartment by myself, and surprisingly, I'm still there. I've survived a fire in the kitchen (totally not my fault), a flood (OK, my fault), a broken refrigerator, two roommates, kitten births and deaths, and having (and losing) the love of my life. I knew it wouldn't be easy, but I just didn't think it would be this hard.

When you're in care, you think that leaving care is going to make all your problems go away. What you don't realize is how you'll have a whole set of new ones.

There are days when I want to move back to the apartment program for mentally ill adults, where I was at least partly taken care of. Some days I just want to stay underneath the covers because facing each day means buying cat food, or having to replace another light bulb, or harassing the landlord to finally fix my bathroom sink. Some days I wonder if all the fighting I did to become independent was even worth it.

But then there are days when I look around and just go, "Wow," because this apartment and this life is mine. I've created it. For better or for worse (or until the end of my lease) it's all mine and I will fight to the death to keep it. And now I can see how getting here—to a place where I'm more or less independent—required me to be brave enough to accept help, and to let myself actually depend a bit on people who could help me.

When I think about that, I think that no one is really ever completely independent, and who would want to be? Knowing how to help and be helped by others is part of being an adult.

Too Much Pride

I learned that asking for help isn't weak.

By ANTWAUN GARCIA

I come from a family with a huge amount of pride. The men in my family especially have a lot of pride and don't like to ask for help. So until recently I rarely asked for help. I was scared of being looked upon as less of a man.

Antwaun Garcia

I guess that's because I used to always feel that people were against me. I felt this because so many people I was close to said I would never succeed. They said I would turn out just like my father. I felt they were just trying to break me and put me down. I told myself I would have to succeed without anyone's help just to prove them wrong.

My Pride Got Me in Trouble

But sometimes my pride and my determination to do things without help got me in trouble. I was one of those kids who was quick to fight. I had a couple of fights where other dudes pulled out knives on me, and I still fought them. It made me feel strong and independent, like I was grown enough to handle it on my own. But looking back, that wasn't too smart. What if I got into a fight with the wrong person and he pulled a gun? I don't think my pride would have helped me out.

Still, my pride grew and stayed with me throughout my teenage years. I taught myself how to play basketball, how to talk to females, and how to make my own judgments. I almost never asked my aunt, who I live with, for spending money. With everything I did, I challenged myself to be the best and told myself that the best always stand alone. I thought that if I asked for help it would look as though I succeeded because of that help, not because of all my work and determination.

Emotions With Nowhere to Go

I also almost never talked to anyone about my feelings, even though I had been through a lot in life and it weighed on me. Instead, I let out my emotions with a pen and a pad. And that worked fine until I got to the point where I faced things I couldn't understand. I had questions like: Why was I ever put in foster care? Why did my parents abandon me? Why do I feel alone? The older I became the more things were unclear.

I had so many questions and no answers, and my pen and pad couldn't answer them, because I was the one writing.

Social workers and my friends sometimes said I should see a therapist to help me deal. But I felt that if I went to a therapist for help, it would make me soft or weak. So even though I wanted so badly to ask for help, I just couldn't bring myself to do it. I was left with hundreds of questions.

I Went to My Brother

Then I had a problem with my ex, and I didn't know what to do. It was driving me crazy. So I decided to go to my brother Mel. Mel had a wifey he had been with on and off for almost 10 years, so there was no one better to ask than him.

At first I was hesitant, because I didn't want my brother knowing my business like that. We were always cool back in the day, but since we hadn't really kept in contact for five years, I didn't know whether I should go to him or not.

> **It feels good to know that I can rely on people once in a blue.**

I took a chance. I asked him for some advice, not having any high hopes of how it would go. But from the start of the convo, we got into it. Personal feelings about this, that and the third. I mean, he even helped me out in situations that I may encounter later on in life with a female. So it worked out better than I ever expected. And it felt cool to see I could fall back on my fam to help me out.

It Feels Good to Depend on Others

It didn't really change my feeling that the world is against me, but I do now feel that I have some people who I can trust.

I'm also realizing that when I leave care I'm going to need people I can depend on. There's so much I need to learn about living independently before I age out. I need to learn about getting an apartment, paying bills and saving money, to name a few things, and I need to learn those things fast. So it's finally hitting me that it don't make me less of a man but more of a person to know when I need help.

And you know what? It feels good to know that I can rely on people once in a blue. And it feels good getting to know my family again.

Think About It:

Remember a time you asked for help from someone. How did you feel asking for help?

_____

_____

_____

Did you get the help you needed? _____

_____

_____

_____

In general, is it easy or difficult for you to ask for help from others? If it's difficult, what can you do to make it more comfortable?

_____

_____

_____

An Emotional Rollercoaster

A former foster child turned expert discusses how to prepare for life's challenges, starting from inside.

By IJEOMA OKOLO

Interview with Gessy Nixon, who grew up in care and now works with youth in care.

Ijeoma Okolo

Throughout my years in foster care, I was depressed. I always thought that if I had this or that, like an apartment or a job or a boyfriend, then I would be happy. But in fact, after I left foster care, I came close to having it all. I had a guy in my life, my own place, an education and a job. But I was still depressed and not emotionally prepared to be on my own.

For example, I would tell my boyfriend all kinds of lies that I thought would make him love me more and more. I told him I was a virgin, which I wasn't. I also did things I didn't want to do with him to keep him, like cooking for him, having sex with him when I didn't want to, and hating whoever he hated.

I Wasn't Emotionally Ready for Independence

Eventually I did not want to lie anymore, and we broke up.

Also, with jobs, whenever a problem came up, I did not try to work it out. I just quit. Again, I was just not emotionally prepared to hold down a job.

In foster care, people talk about success as achieving things, like having a job, money, your own place, and an education. We forget about how important it is to be prepared emotionally for life on our own.

The Pain of Our Pasts Comes With Us

Not only do a lot of us feel very lonely when we first leave foster care, we also realize that some of the pain from our pasts doesn't go away just because we're out of the system. Many of us came into care because we were abused or lost a parent. Sometimes we try to veil this hurt. Then when we're on our own, we come face to face with the pain of our pasts.

Gessy Nixon

But how can young people leaving foster care become more emotionally able to face life's challenges? Gessy Nixon, a former foster child and cofounder of Voices of Youth, which trains young people in foster care to speak out about their experiences, gave me her thoughts on how teens in care can better prepare themselves to emotionally handle life after care.

What is your definition of a person who successfully left foster care?

Answer: Success is different depending on the person. For me, when I left care, success was having a roof over my head and something to eat. For other people success is getting a GED or graduating from college and proving your parent, who said you weren't going to be anything, wrong. Or it may be seeing that your brothers and sisters are living in the same place.

Young people who are successful tend to look at the outside things—that they graduated from school, that they're working—but they forget that they are still struggling to survive on the inside. Once you have a place to sleep and eat, all the emotions on the inside come up, like fear and anger and loneliness.

Sometimes your parent, the person you most want approval from, doesn't give you approval so you don't feel successful no matter what you accomplish.

What does it take to be fully prepared to live life after care?

Answer: Being prepared to be on your own and to face life is more than just having a job, a car or education. It's also about being mentally and emotionally prepared.

Not dealing with emotional issues can affect a young person. A lot of young people can't deal with conflict so when they have a boss who gets on their nerves, they'll quit the job instead of working through it. Or if they get yelled at they'll respond in a negative way instead of learning a different way.

And when you haven't had a say so in your life, you aren't prepared to make decisions because you have never had a chance to make decisions and fail and learn from them.

If young people have a job, go to school, learn decision-making, have some healthy adults in their life and have a sense of who they are, I think they'll do better. They should have a couple of people, at least two or three, that they can go to without feeling judged. These should be people who can give good advice, and who the teens have nothing to gain or lose from telling them about their problems. They need someone who can help them see their options, so they can make decisions for themselves. Ultimately the person who has to live with the decision is the young person.

> **'Succeeding after care comes down to what you do at night when you're all alone and lonely, or when you're depressed, and how you deal with that.'**

But succeeding after care comes down to what do you do at night when you're all alone and lonely, or when you're depressed, and how you deal with that. Young people have to know how to get through that. They have to know that they have gifts, talents and abilities to offer. They have to have a sense of who they are and how to make decisions—so, for instance, they don't take the worst boyfriend in the world. A lot of girls are making decisions that are life threatening because they don't know who they are.

And if you don't feel worthy you aren't going to ask a teacher for help. You aren't going to go knocking down the doors of an employer, telling them they should hire you.

Another important thing for a young person to have is a sense of hope, and that everything will be all right. If you don't have that you can be crushed if you get fired from a job or your friends don't call you or your boyfriend leaves you. You need a sense of believing that you can get through this and you can get through tomorrow. Without that things feel overwhelming or impossible and you spend a lot of time being fearful.

> **'You do want to deal with your pain at some point, because you don't want to pass that stuff on to your children or your relationships.'**

The one thing you can have is who you believe you are and how you see yourself and confidence. That nobody can steal. That's what's going to keep you going and give you a sense of joy and peace no matter where you go.

Do you think teens in care should go to therapy to help them deal with leaving care?

Answer: It depends where you're at. If you're emotionally ready to deal with the past, then deal with it. I used to have nightmares a lot about something that happened to me as a child but I wasn't ready to deal with that thing until I was married and had children. I couldn't have dealt with it as a teen because it would have crushed me, but when I was an adult and had support in my life it felt OK to deal with the past.

But you do want to deal with your pain at some point, because you don't want to pass that stuff onto your children or your relationships. And you don't want to store it up and have it explode in long periods of depression or destructiveness.

Any last thoughts on the emotional challenges of leaving care?

Answer: I'm glad to hear someone is talking about it because I think it's hard for adults to deal with the emotional side of aging out, so they just don't. But ultimately, learning how to budget and cook and all those other independent living skills is the easy stuff to learn. The emotional stuff is the deeper stuff. There are so many people who look just fine on the outside but at the holidays they try to commit suicide, or lock themselves in the house depressed, or they go from job to job because they can't deal with conflict, or they get in abusive relationships. It's important to try to deal with your emotional issues when you feel you can.

If you don't deal with it, it's going to come out in your relationships anyway. When you have children it can cause you to be stressed and say things and do things you don't want to do. It will also come out in yourself—how you treat yourself, how you dress, what kind of jobs you choose. The pain of the past is in you and it's going to come out no matter what. You want it to come out safely and in a way you can deal with.

Psych! How to Know When to Seek Out Therapy

By DOMINICK FREEMAN

Therapy has helped all kinds of people—including me!—with their problems. In my case, therapy helped me to see patterns I had that were not helping me be happy, so I could change them.

I've found that therapy helps me live my every day life and put up with people who are mean, annoying or just down-right stupid. It helps to have someone show me how to cope with problems so I can choose my own fate.

There are some situations, though, when you should see a therapist, such as when you're dealing with life-threatening issues.

Here are some instances in which you should seek the help of a mental health professional, even if you don't feel like it:

■ When you are thinking about killing or hurting yourself or someone else.

■ If you worry all the time about your weight, have problems with anorexia or bulimia, or can't stop eating.

■ When you cannot stop drinking or taking drugs, or when your drug and alcohol use is messing up the rest of your life.

■ When you act in dangerous ways or find yourself on either side of an abusive relationship.

■ If you are like a walking time bomb, and find yourself flipping out and angry or sad most of the time.

■ When you dwell on traumatic experiences or your bad childhood and can't get these thoughts out of your mind.

■ When you feel so overworked, depressed or overstressed you can't do the things you need to, like go to school, complete your homework, do your chores, or see your friends.

■ When you have nightmares or thoughts that don't let you sleep.

■ If you hear voices and see things that other people don't hear or see.

So many people are trapped in lives of misery and pain. Not one of us should have to live that way. Therapy can help.

I Left Foster Care but My Past Came With Me

By MARY HANSON

One day when I was 25, I sat in church reading the Sunday bulletin. I noticed there was a brunch at one of Houston's yuppie restaurants. I was hungry, and I wanted to meet new people. But I was nervous and scared. I got on the freeway, got off the freeway, and circled around for 15 minutes.

"OK, this is ridiculous, either go or don't go," I told myself. I felt pressure to go because I had decided not long before to leave my circle of unhealthy friendships and find people who could be positive for me.

Finally I drove to the restaurant. I took a deep breath and walked over to the group of people from my church. Gene, a guy with sandy-colored hair and a medium build, came over to talk to me. In the restaurant, Gene sat next to me.

A Different Kind of Guy

We talked non-stop as if no one else was around, and after that we started dating. On our first date, to the beach, I told him about my parents, who were mentally retarded, and my 12 years in foster care as if I was attempting to run him off. He didn't run away. He called me and asked me out again. I knew then that he was different.

When Gene and I started to date, I made the decision to start emotionally taking care of myself. I'd started to realize that I couldn't close the door on 12 years in foster care as if they never happened. Time had healed nothing. Ten years later, I was angry as the day I left foster care.

When I began reflecting on my years in foster care, I realized why I was having trouble standing alone, being confident and accepting myself.

In my foster homes, I was rejected so many times that I actually began to believe I was bad and unlovable. I believed that it was my fault that I was moved from home to home. I believed that if I hadn't been so bad the foster parents would have kept me.

In reality I was a normal kid who did normal things.

But I learned that by pleasing people, I could get affirmation and security. So I tried to fit into everyone else's world and get everyone else to like me. I got pushed around and felt unable to stand up for myself.

Do You Have What It Takes?

Foster care also didn't give me the increasing responsibilities that I might have had in a good family. Before I left care at 15, I'd never been allowed to make a decision for myself. The system then sent me to live with my aunt, and there I had to make all my own decisions.

My aunt expected me to feed and clothe myself, so I had to earn a living. She paid no attention to me, so I had to figure out how I wanted to live. My low grades reflected these adult responsibilities. Three years later, I barely graduated high school.

I Tried to Put Foster Care in the Past

Still, after graduating from high school, I thought I had a fairly easy transition to adult life. For the first time I was in control of my life. It felt great. I decided to work and put all my years of foster care in the past.

> **I began to realize that my past kept popping in my head like those Internet pop-up ads. I perceived every minor violation as a World War III attack.**

I thought all the sadness and anger I felt in foster care would be behind me. But in truth, I was extremely lonely, feeling helpless and out of control. I felt insecure and questioned every decision I made. I had no one to turn to so if I met anyone who I thought could help me, I asked them about making it on my own. I got a lot of practical help, and throughout my 20s I worked steadily and lived on my own. But professional success didn't make me happy. Instead, I was miserable but successful.

In my early 20s, I worked as a flight attendant and lived far from family. As a flight attendant I was used to being treated with respect. I didn't realize until I quit my job and moved back to Houston just how badly my old friends and family had been treating me.

When I got back, I learned that my family had stolen things out of my storage unit and sold them in a garage sale. I was furious. How could they sell my things and keep the money?

My Past Kept Popping Up

I began to realize that my past kept popping in my head like those Internet pop-up ads. I perceived every minor violation as a World War III attack and felt like I had to defend myself. I would go into a rage and then fill up with tears, depression and a deep hurt.

Repressing my feelings had helped me become a successful professional. But I had stopped being able to control the force of resentment and anger that surfaced whenever I felt like I was being treated unfairly.

Therapist #1: A Quick Fix

Finally, I had no choice but to make a visit to the psychologist. She said I needed to set healthy boundaries. That meant that I needed to do what I wanted for myself, and not allow people to treat me in ways that hurt me.

With the help of therapy, I began to stop allowing my family to lean on me. When my aunt had drinking and drug socials, I said I had to work. When my dad asked me for money, I angrily said, "What makes you think I have money?" I shrugged off their guilt trips and did what was in my own best interest.

Then I almost died of a brain aneurysm. It was terrifying, but it forced me to change so much about myself. As I lay in the hospital, I had to recognize that none of my family came to see me. I was numb. Over night I changed my priorities. I stopped smoking and drinking. I told myself that my family had never been there except to ridicule or use me. I had no choice but to see them for who they were.

I only went to counseling long enough to get out of my crisis. I didn't have the time, money or energy to continue. Long-term therapy is emotionally taxing. I got my quick fix, got out of a major depression and tried to move on with my life.

W hile working at a nightclub in Houston I ran into an old acquaintance named Mark. We started to date, but the more I got to know him, the more I did not like what I saw. He was a jeweler and his employer claimed he was missing jewelry. He didn't pay rent because he was fixing up the landlady's apartment—until she realized he was taking advantage. Then he got a job at a bar and got fired for coming up short of money on the register.

One night he became angry with me and took my hand and pounded it into my forehead. That was it. Our relationship was over. He didn't accept the breakup, calling me at work and begging forgiveness five, six times in a row. I feared losing my job because he was harassing. I didn't back down, but the experience left me shaken and depressed.

> **I've come to realize that the best thing I can do is stop the dysfunction that has run in my family for so long.**

Therapist #2: I Blew Her Doors Off

I picked one of the therapists on my insurance plan and went to her office upset but composed. She was a frail, thin, older lady that reminded me of someone's mother. I blurted out everything and she looked at me. She said, "Oh my God," and started grabbing papers on codependency, addiction, trust, anger, depression and anxiety. I left her office and never went back. I thought, "This lady can't handle me! I just blew her doors off."

Therapist #3: Stop Dating Jerks

One Saturday I was driving around crying hysterically, thinking about suicide. I decided to try counseling again. I knew if I was that depressed I had a problem.

I wanted to know from my therapist why only unhealthy guys were asking me out. My therapist told me, "By accepting a date you're choosing them." This was a revelation to me: Who I dated was my choice.

I felt inspired and empowered.

I stopped therapy after three months, but it definitely helped. I soon met a guy who, after one date, wanted too much from me. I never saw him again. Then a guy asked me to meet him for cocktails. After one drink he asked me to go to his house for dinner. I said, "I'd rather get dinner in a restaurant." He got angry. I never saw him again, either.

Finding Mr. Right

That's when I decided to start going to church again. And that's how I met Gene. In Gene, I knew I had found someone who could truly be a husband and a father. He was calm and patient with me. He was sensitive and we talked about everything. He also supported me by helping me to pursue my interests in school.

Gene expanded my interests. He took me skiing three years in a row, and even got me lessons and clothes to wear for our trip. We ran a marathon together. And once he asked me to a ball and then bought me a dress to wear because I didn't have one. We were in love and our times together were fun.

But after we'd been dating for three years, he broke up with me, saying he was unable to decide if he wanted to make a commitment. I was angry and hurt. I didn't understand how someone could possibly not know what he wanted. Angrily, I said, "Figure it out."

Therapist #4: Commit to Him

I ended up at the psychologist again because I was feeling insecure and I didn't know what to do. Gene was the man I wanted to marry.

I told the therapist that I'd already bought him a Christmas present, spending more than I could afford on a midnight blue cashmere sweater I thought he'd like. I didn't know what to do with it. The psychologist told me to do what my heart told me. I gave Gene the sweater. After Christmas we started dating again and one year later he asked me to marry him. He told me later that when we broke up he realized what he'd lost.

Therapist #5: 'You Can't Control Others'

Getting married and dealing with my new in-laws brought back negative feelings from childhood. I'd always dreamt I'd marry a guy with a loving family. But his family rejected me, saying, "I'm worried about where you came from." When they said that, an intense rage came over me. I felt judged by the past I'd tried so hard to overcome. And I felt irrationally afraid that I'd end up getting abused again.

After a honeymoon stuffing all my emotions inside me, my husband and I headed for therapy. The therapist pointed out to my husband and me that in-law problems like this happen all the time, but that I was experiencing intense rage, anger and hurt because the rejection was a replay of my foster care experiences.

She helped me see that although I wasn't causing the problems, I wasn't handling rejection well either. Their cruelness towards me is about them. If Gene had married someone else, they would've treated her badly, too. I learned that I cannot control others and their actions, but I can control mine.

Therapist #6: As Angry as Ever

When we moved from Houston to Wyoming, I screamed at the realtor. I was unable to tolerate her incompetence. That landed me in therapy once again because I knew raging at a realtor wasn't acceptable.

Therapist #7: I Need this Long-Term

I thought I was done with therapy! But when my husband and I planned a trip to visit his parents, every negative thought possible came into my mind. I started to toss and turn all night.

Then I thought, "I can't handle this. I won't go through it again. I should kill myself." I started to drink, not to calm myself but to be self-destructive.

When my mother-in-law called, I panicked. Trying to think of the quickest way to get my point across, I said, "I have a little bit of post-traumatic stress going on here." Then I told her, "You have no right to judge my parents. I didn't come from anywhere you didn't." I started to weep and said, "I've got to go."

Stopping the Dysfunction

Finally, I realized that I needed long-term therapy to address the root causes of my pain and anger. Twelve years in foster care would not be erased with occasional, brief psychotherapy.

I've come to realize that the best thing I can do is stop the dysfunction that has run in my family for so long. It is my intention to be the best possible mother.

Forgiveness is still a struggle. I know I need to heal my wounds but it's not easy. I am relieved that therapy has enabled me to label my feelings. That helps me deal with my pain. Unfortunately, at times the song of my past takes over. I rage, become unable to think, drink in excess, have flashbacks and get to the point of thinking about suicide.

Finally Dealing With My Past

When I first went to counseling, the therapist gave me some information about psychological problems I was dealing with. The information was overwhelming so I filed it away.

Now, ten years later, I still pull out all the sheets of paper. I'm overwhelmed to see that they knew all along what was going on with me. I wasn't ready to deal with it all. I've only dealt with each situation as it became important in my life to do that.

I've come a long way psychologically. I've been out of foster care for 22 years. I'm still amazed by its long series of after-effects that continue to control my life.

Creating My Own Family

The first time I went to therapy I told the therapist about my aunt's mental abuse. Instead of helping me, that therapist told my aunt everything and I got in trouble. So when I entered the system, I didn't trust therapists. I trusted them less after all the ones I saw in the system wanted to put me on medication. I felt like they weren't trying to understand what I went through as a child.

Now I'm an adult and a mother. I am not in foster care but I am still living like I am. I still move around, but now I don't have a system to run to every time I get in trouble. So I am trying to learn to create my own system of family and anyone who is positive to support me and help me reach my dreams.

To do this, I have found that I have to finally deal with my demons.

It's funny. When I was a child all I wanted to do was grow up. Now that I'm grown up, all I want to do is take care of myself. And I want to open up my own business. To do that, I am dealing with my past. I am talking to a therapist and I am also receiving counseling in church so that I can finally move on and stay on the right road to my dreams.

In the system, I was always so busy helping everyone else that I forgot about what Youniqiue (that's me) wants and how Youniqiue plans on getting it. Now I am working on finding those things out.

—Youniqiue Symone

Activity Page for Group Leaders

Identifying a Support Network

Topic: Identifying a support network

Goal: Help teens identify who they can turn to for help and support after they leave care

Time: 1 hour

What you'll need: Construction paper, pens, stapler

Read story: 15 minutes

■ **Tell teens:** "We're going to read a story about a young woman who left care to live on her own. Every time the writer talks about a person who helped or supported her in some way, we'll stop reading and we'll write their name on the board."

■ **Read "Phoenix Rising"** on p. 120 out loud

Discussion: 15 minutes

■ **Tell group:** "On a piece of paper, list all the situations you think you might need help with. List all the people you can ask for help in different situations."

■ **Ask group and discuss:** What are some situations you think you might need help with? (List these on the board.) Who do you think you could turn to for help in each situation? What do you think you could ask them for? What do you think you could not ask them for? (Make sure you use yourself as an example of someone they can ask for help on some things, but probably not everything.)

Activity: 15 minutes

■ **Pass out pens and construction paper.**

■ **Have group make their own personal "little black books"** of people they can count on or a "wish list" of people they'd like to be able to count on for the various situations listed on the board. Tell the students to list the people's contact information and why/how they're helpful. They can slao use the worksheet on p. 147 for this.

Closing discussion: 10 minutes

■ **Ask group:** How can you get closer to the people that you know? How can you find more people to be part of your support network?

■ **Tell groups** that being independent includes having the support and help of other people. Part of preparing for independence requires building a support network of people who teens can turn to as they forge a life outside the foster care system.

My Support System

List all the people who you can turn to for advice, help, or company in each situation. Be sure to consider adults in your life, like family and relatives, teachers, social workers, relatives, etc. If you can't think of anyone for a section, make an effort to find someone who can fill that role.

Who can I call for help if I have a medical emergency, for instance, I break a bone or get the flu and need someone to bring me groceries, etc?

1. Name: _____

   Phone number: _____

2. Name: _____

   Phone number: _____

Who can I call if I'm feeling lonely and just want to have fun?

1. Name: _____

   Phone number: _____

2. Name: _____

   Phone number: _____

Do You Have What It Takes?

Who can I call if I need to talk about a personal problem?

1. Name: _____

   Phone number: _____

2. Name: _____

   Phone number: _____

Who can I call if I need to borrow money?

1. Name: _____

   Phone number: _____

2. Name: _____

   Phone number: _____

Who can I call if I need advice on something to do with my job, like how to write a resume, handle a handle a conflict at work, or ask for a raise?

1. Name: _____

   Phone number: _____

2. Name: _____

Phone number: _____

Who can I call if I need advice on educational opportunities, like applying for college or finding a good job training program?

1. Name: _____

Phone number: _____

2. Name: _____

Phone number: _____

Who can I call if I have a question with something around the house, like cooking or cleaning?

1. Name: _____

Phone number: _____

2. Name: _____

Phone number: _____

www.youthcomm.org

Do You Have What It Takes?

Who can I stay with if I need a place to live for a few weeks while I get back on my feet?

1. Name: _____

   Phone number: _____

2. Name: _____

   Phone number: _____

Show your appreciation to these people for being there for you. Everyone needs people to count on and these are the people who are there for you.

Chapter 5

Taking Care of Number One—Health and Hygiene

Taking Care of Number One: Why This Chapter Matters

Last year when I went to the doctor for a physical, he taught me how to check my testicles every month for lumps that might mean I have a hernia, or even cancer. I never knew that such a simple self-exam could save my life!

As we get older, we have to become more responsible about taking care of ourselves in all kinds of new ways. I already drink a lot of water and try to walk from point A to point B to stay in shape. This came in handy when I recently had to run seven blocks to catch a bus because I'd left my wallet on it. (I got it back, too!)

Good health isn't just about taking care of our organs and our outsides. We have to take care of our insides, too, so I go to therapy every week to get my anger under control and learn how to get along better with people.

Keeping ourselves up is especially important for youth in care because we don't have parents taking care of us. We are judged enough by society, and we don't need to be looked down on for not taking care of our hygiene or our medical and dental needs.

Good health habits show courtesy to others and help us be strong and look young, even when we get old. But I've found out that taking care of myself also makes me feel good. I feel so much better when I do things to make myself healthy or that make me look better. I think good habits are therapeutic. We have to love ourselves and be our own best friends.

If we don't love ourselves, who else will?

—Dominick Freeman

Soap Opera: How to Stay Fresh

By KAREEM BANKS

Personal hygiene becomes more important once you hit puberty. Why? The physical changes that happen when we become teenagers result in increased sweat and oil production, which in turn result in…odors. We all know someone with a bad odor problem. You don't like to be around that person, do you? So if you want people to be around you, you have to practice good personal hygiene.

Kareem Banks

1. Wash Yourself Daily

Taking one bath or shower a day is mandatory once your body starts going through these changes. In the summer, when I play a lot of basketball, I may take three showers a day to stay fresh.

When washing up, wet a washrag and rub it with soap until the washcloth is full of soap suds. Then wipe it all over your body in a circular motion, concentrating on your armpits, feet and crotch, where the worst odors come from. My favorite soaps are Irish Spring Sport and Dove. If soap makes your skin dry and ashy, use a mild soap like Dove and moisturize with lotion or Vaseline, especially on your arms and legs. I like to use Baby Magic.

> **All the clothes in the world can look good the first time you wear them, but if you can't keep them clean they're not going to look good for long.**

2. Clean Your Crowning Glory

You also have to shampoo your hair at least once a week, and up to every day if it's oily or fine. If you have dandruff, you should use a dandruff shampoo like Selsun Blue or Head and Shoulders. Conditioner, which you put on and rinse off after rinsing out shampoo, helps moisturize your hair and makes it easier to style.

3. Extra Fresheners

If you use colognes and perfumes, use them only after you shower. They shouldn't be there to disguise the fact you haven't showered! (But because mosquitoes love sweet smells, you may intend to attract people to you with your scent, but wind up attracting a lot of mosquitoes.)

4. Wash Those Hands!

Don't forget to wash your hands every time after you go to the bathroom, handle a pet or litter box, or touch sick people. You should also soap up and rinse off your hands before you prepare food.

5. Wash What You Wear

Keep your clothes as clean as you keep your body. Change into fresh underwear and socks every day. It's OK to wear the same shirt or pair of pants a few times if you haven't gotten them dirty, but after wearing anything for two days, it should be washed.

I do my laundry every Sunday so I have fresh clean clothes at the beginning of every week. Tide is my favorite detergent and I like to use Downy Fabric softener to make my clothes smell good.

It's good to keep clean. It's your body, so take care of it!

Flossed Out:
How to Keep Your Teeth Clean

By TABITHA KOZAKIEWICZ

Do you know the dirtiest area of your body?

Inside your mouth!

The bacteria in your mouth is so powerful that it produces acids that attack and break down your teeth and gums.

Tabitha Kozakiewicz

Most of us were taught in elementary school that it's important to brush, eat right and floss to prevent cavities, yellow teeth, bad breath and gum disease. Still, we often ignore this advice because we're young. It's hard to imagine that our teeth will rot and fall out years from now if we don't take care of them today.

> **I won't even date anyone who doesn't floss. My mouth is too clean to kiss a bacteria-infested mouth!**

Advertising tells us we can have healthy teeth without spending any time to keep them that way. Listerine's label says it is "as effective as floss." At first, I believed this! But I researched this claim and found that while mouthwashes may kill off some bacteria, only flossing prevents gum disease, which can make your teeth fall out and your breath stink. If you're pregnant, gum disease can make it more likely that you'll miscarry or deliver your baby early. Gum disease can even kill you. How? By setting off blood clots that lead to stroke and heart attacks.

Liquids can't get out the leftover food and bacteria stuck between the teeth. If that stuff is left in there, the bacteria multiply and eventually you get gingivitis—the first stage of gum disease. Also, flossing takes off plaque and prevents your teeth from yellowing.

When I learned how important flossing was, I decided I didn't want to get gum disease or wind up spending thousands of dollars on fillings, crowns, oral surgery and even implants or dentures. So I started flossing every day.

Now I won't even date anyone who doesn't floss. My mouth and teeth are too clean to kiss a bacteria-infested mouth.

Let me give you the 411 on oral hygiene 101:

1. Brush After Every Meal, or, at the minimum, every

morning after breakfast and every night before you go to bed, with a toothpaste that contains fluoride. Use a soft-bristled brush, and brush your teeth at an angle. Use back-and-forth and round motions, getting all sides and chewing surfaces, including the back side of your last molars. Finally, brush your tongue to remove bacteria and freshen breath. Spend at least two full minutes brushing your teeth. Buy a new toothbrush every three months.

2. Try to Floss after Every Meal, but if you can't,

at least floss at the end of every single day. Here's how: Pull off about 18 inches of floss, and use it to form a "C" shape on your tooth. Gently rub it up and down the side of each tooth, making sure you don't ram your gums. Instead, go gently between the gum and the tooth. Do every side of every single tooth.

3. Get Your Teeth Deep-cleaned

Professionally every six months and see a dentist regularly to

keep your cavities filled and teeth healthy. If you've aged out and can't afford a dentist, check out the dental schools at universities near you. Dental schools have programs where a student who is supervised by a teacher can give you dental care.

Celebrities have made teeth bleaching popular, but before you decide to do it, you should ask your dentist. Your teeth might be too sensitive to tolerate bleaching.

Now smile!

Natural Woman

Skin care products you can make at home.

By PAULINE GORDON

When puberty hit, thousands of pimples invaded my face. I tried so many different products that promised me perfection. They only made my skin feel extremely dry.

One night I went to bed with a burning sensation on my face. Silly me, I ignored it and woke up to discover that my face had become so raw and irritated it was bleeding.

Pauline Gordon

Finally, I stopped abusing my skin and dropping my money on all those harsh chemicals. Instead, I drank lots of water, stayed away from sweets and stopped applying a bunch of junk to my face. My acne calmed down.

Sweet Papaya and Mango Lotions

Then, last year, I attended a fair in Kentucky. The aroma of sugar and vanilla, sweet papaya and mango lured me to a tent filled with organic skin care products. I tried out each one, rubbing the lotions into my skin and smelling the soaps.

The owner liked my reaction and introduced herself to me. She told me that making skin care products was her hobby, and that she preferred washing with natural ingredients like oatmeal and honey.

When I got back to New York, I searched the web for skin care products I could make at home. I found a site called www.honey.com, which was filled with recipes for lotions and scrubs. I was thrilled.

Cooking Up Scrubs

Making the natural products was fun. First I bought some unusual ingredients—like vitamin E oil and wheat germ—and some more typical things, like almonds, coffee and cucumber. Then I followed the recipes, just like I was cooking. I washed and peeled some cucumbers for the

Cucumber Skin Toner, then dropped oatmeal and almonds in the mixer.

I enjoyed mixing and grinding the ingredients. Gripping a handful of honey and oatmeal in my palms, I devoured the sweet aroma. I grew tempted to actually devour it! But I tried my best not to eat the skin care products.

When finished, I stored each freshly made product in its own container. The next morning, they would be ready to use.

Morning Buzz Kill

When the morning sunrise awakened me, I reached past the store-bought products in the cabinet, my fingers tracing each of the labels and stopping on the one marked Morning Buzz Body Scrub.

This one was made with freshly ground coffee, honey and grapeseed oil. I wondered, "What effect could ground coffee possibly have on skin?" As I let the warm water run in the shower, I scrubbed it against my skin.

In seconds, I looked as if I was rolling around in dirt. I got nervous about letting the coffee near my private parts, and wasn't sure whether to use soap, too. Dismayed by my first experience with my homemade products, I immediately rinsed off and showered with soap.

A Rodeo in the Bathroom

Minutes later, I was startled to hear my grandmother ranting and raving. When I came back into the bathroom, she looked astounded. "Pauline, if I'd known you were that dirty, I would have sprayed you with the hose," she said.

I was confused for a minute, then remembered the body scrub and looked behind her to a dreadful scene. Our bathroom that's usually washed down with bleach was smothered with coffee grounds. It looked like a rodeo had taken place in my shower. Disgusted, I immediately threw the container of Morning Buzz Scrub away, vowing never to use it again.

Fresh and Clean

Luckily, my other products came out much better. The cucumber toner felt light and gentle, and I loved how the Honey Almond Scrub felt. It was sweet smelling but rough against my face, and after I rinsed the scrub off, I was left with a cool sensation. My face felt fresh and clean.

It felt good to know exactly what I was putting on my face, and to use natural ingredients, instead of the dozens of strange chemicals listed on the back of most products. Morning Buzz was a disaster, but the other products were my reward.

Inner Beauty

What you eat affects how you look.

By PAULINE GORDON

Just about every teenager gazes at herself in the mirror, worrying about things like thin hair, pimples or nails that just don't grow. Instead of reaching for whatever sensational new product you see in the pharmacy, consider the role your diet plays in your appearance. Healthy skin, hair and nails start with what you eat.

Pauline Gordon

To find out how to maintain a healthy body, inside and out, I interviewed Rebecca Berman, a nutritionist at Northwestern University in Evanston, Illinois.

How do you keep hair, skin and nails healthy?

Answer: It's important to eat a balanced diet. That means eating fruits, vegetables and whole grains like whole wheat bread and brown rice. Iron is one of the more important nutrients for strong nails and hair. Iron is found in foods like red meat (beef), green vegetables, dry seeds and enriched cereals.

One sign of iron deficiency or anemia is when your nails kind of curl up, giving them the shape of an upturned spoon. Getting enough iron in your diet can correct that.

Vitamin B also strengthens nails. Vitamin B is in dairy products, vegetables, nuts like walnuts or almonds, and tuna.

If you lose a lot of weight quickly or go on a crash diet, you might develop horizontal lines or ridges in your nails. Also, your hair can fall out. I see young ladies on drastic diets who complain about hair falling out or thinning.

If you want a nice glossy head of hair, and healthy skin and nails, you want to make sure you have some healthy fats, like olive oil or canola oil, in your diet. If you restrict the fat in your diet too much, you don't produce enough estrogen, and that shows in your hair, nails and skin.

Another way to protect hair, skin and nails is to make sure you're getting enough fluid, staying hydrated. Each day drink about eight 8 oz. glasses of water or juice—not liquids that have alcohol or caffeine.

Which is a healthier way to get vitamins, through supplements or by eating food?

Answer: It's best to get your vitamins from foods, mainly because there are other substances in foods that work with vitamins and minerals to protect us against diseases and keep us healthy.

What are antioxidants?

Answer: These are substances found in foods, especially fruits and vegetables and tea, which may play a role in combating certain illnesses, like cancer. They help to prevent a cancerous cell from developing into a tumor. It's also thought that they might protect from heart disease, and that people who eat a lot of antioxidants suffer less damage to their skin.

Are juices as good for you as vegetables or fruits?

Answer: In terms of vitamin or mineral content, yes. But in fresh vegetables and fruits there's fiber. Fiber helps with digestion. It controls and stabilizes your blood sugar and gives you the feeling of fullness. Try to eat your fruits and vegetables rather than drink them. A 4 oz glass of orange juice has the same calories as a small orange, but an orange will make you feel fuller.

Do certain foods cause breakouts?

Answer: Acne is caused mostly by hormones. It's still up in the air whether specific foods cause or aggravate acne. If you find that chocolate or greasy foods aggravate your acne, stop eating them. You don't need those foods anyway.

www.youthcomm.org

Activity Page for Group Leaders

Making a Self-Care Plan

> **Topic:** Making a self-care plan
>
> **Goal:** Help teens make a self-care plan can help teens cement healthy habits before they leave the system. It will also give them a guide to refer to in emergencies, or as a reminder to get check-ups at the doctor or dentist.
>
> **Time:** 1 hour and 15 minutes

Lesson: 1 hour

The stories in this chapter describe how to take care of basic and emergency health needs, like showering daily and taking care of your teeth. You can use these stories to get teens talking about topics they might feel squeamish or corny discussing, like flossing or using deodorant.

■ **Read silently or aloud:** Split your class into groups and ask each group to read a story of their choice from this chapter. They can read them out loud or silently.

  1) Ask the teens to underline sentences where the writer explains the consequences of not taking care of yourself, like cavities.

  2) Ask them to circle all of the ways the writer suggests taking care of yourself, like flossing daily.

■ **Discuss:** Ask each person to tell the group one new thing she learned from the article, or one thing that other teens in the room might need to know. Your teens may disagree on a few points ("Is it necessary to wash shirts after every wearing?"). Encourage them to talk through any disagreements.

Ask the group, "Are there any suggestions the writers didn't make that you'd add?" This gives them a chance to show their own expertise. Also ask them, "Are there other topics that the chapter could have included?" (When to see an eye doctor, for example, or how to take care of your hair on a tight budget.) They can use the worksheets on p. 163 and 164 to make their plan.

Activity: 15 minutes

■ **Write on the board:** "Self-Care Plan: Daily—Weekly—Yearly—In Emergencies" Ask the teens in your group to list each activity that they should do for each category, including any topics that came up in the discussion that the chapter did not include.

■ **Ask your teens to write down their own Self-Care Plans.** They should include any other aspects of caring for themselves, like taking medicines, seeing specialists, attending weekly therapy, etc.

My Self-Care Plan

TAKING CARE OF YOURSELF INVOLVES:

- ☐ Brushing your teeth
- ☐ Flossing
- ☐ Taking regular showers with soap
- ☐ Getting a doctor's check up, or
- ☐ For females, going to the gynecologist
- ☐ Getting a dental check-up
- ☐ Using deodorant
- ☐ Doing laundry
- ☐ Cleaning your apartment
- ☐ Getting your hair cut or styled

TAKING CARE OF YOURSELF CAN ALSO INVOLVE:

- ☐ Exercising
- ☐ Taking doctor-prescribed medication
- ☐ Therapy
- ☐ Taking vitamins
- ☐ Eating healthy foods and watching your weight

Do You Have What It Takes?

Using the lists on p. 163 with this worksheet, make your own self-care plan. Check off each self-care task from the lists above when you include it in your plan.

Every day, I will: _____

_____

_____

Every week, I will: _____

_____

_____

Every month, I will: _____

_____

_____

Once or twice a year I will: _____

_____

_____

Chapter 6
Keeping House

Keeping House:
Why This Chapter Matters

In the beginning of this book, Ja'Nelle Earle talks about how in her group home residents weren't allowed to cook and staff even did their laundry for them (page 25). Like Ja'Nelle, too often those of us in care don't learn important life skills like cooking and cleaning while we're young because they're done for us. Some might say that's just great...until they're living in their first apartment, on their own.

The stories in this chapter will teach you the joys of keeping a clean crib—cooking, cleaning, and keeping your clothes looking as sharp as writer Kareem Banks keeps his.

A Clean Sweep

My apartment went from nasty to neat.

By CHRISTINE McKENNA

I've been trying to clean my house for about three weeks now. I don't mean that silly straightening up and putting everything away so that the house only looks clean, but still isn't. I mean that scrubbing-the-floors-and-looking-like-Cinderella-as-you-do type of cleaning. I've been living in my own studio apartment for about a year now, and I usually give it a serious cleaning about once a month.

Christine McKenna

But for some reason or another, I hadn't been doing it lately. In fact, I hadn't really cleaned my home in over three months, mainly because of laziness, one of my favorite pastimes.

But it was time to do that down and dirty cleaning. My adventures began.

Use the Broom

Always sweep before you mop. That way you aren't mopping dirt into the floor.

Let it be known that there are three kittens in my house who have not yet learned that the litter box is for them. They much prefer to pee under the nice, warm stove. Gross, I know. And so is the smell. No kidding. It was horrible, so under the stove was the obvious place to start cleaning. (Pets are nice, but they can cause more problems than they are worth.)

Tackling the Kitchen

For me, cleaning the kitchen usually means just washing the dishes, wiping down the cabinets, and sweeping and mopping. When I'm feeling really crazed, cleaning inside the cabinets, and cleaning the stove. Then sweeping and mopping. This time I decided to do all that and attack the smelly mess under the stove.

I started with the dishes. Easy enough. I've seen them pile up worse. I used my generic brand liquid—much cheaper than the advertised brands.

Tests of Strength and Endurance

Next comes under the stove. Man, I was totally trying to put this off, or convince myself that the smell wasn't that bad. It was. I don't know how I ignored it for so long. But I did know that if I ever wanted friends to enter my home again, I'd better clean under the stove.

Who knew that you can't pull the stove all the way out because there's a thick cord and gas line running out of it and into the wall? (And, I later found out, if you have a gas stove, like I do, forcing the stove too far out could damage the gas line, and create a serious fire hazard.)

Keep Bugs Out

Mice and roaches are probably living in your building—don't invite them over to dinner. Clean up crumbs after you eat. Sweep the floor after you cook. Take out garbage before it stinks.

When I figured out I couldn't just slide the stove forward, I stood peering behind of the stove with this dumb look on my face. Then I went into "I Love Lucy" phase. This is where the physical comedy comes in. I got on my knees, tilted the stove back, and tried to balance it on top of my head while sweeping under it at the same time, all the while fearing that at any moment the stove might come crashing down. Don't try this one at home, kids.

Eventually I managed to kick a bucket of water and bleach under the stove. (Bleach is a disinfectant, which means it kills germs. I mix it half and half with water.) While I let the water and bleach soak in, I got up, smoked a cigarette, and gave my cats the evil eye. Then I mopped it up.

Sweeping and Mopping

After tackling the smelly stove, sweeping and mopping the kitchen floor was a cinch. I have wood floors, so I don't want to damage them with harsh chemicals (and lose money from my damage deposit!). So I usually use plain water, or wash with just a little dishwashing soap. But someone told me that Lysol, which is a disinfectant, could be used on floors, too, so I decided to use Lysol. It, uh, kinda worked. My floors were clean, but it had this weird residue on it, so I went over it with some Mop n' Shine. (Mop n' Shine is the generic version of Mop n' Glow, for those of us on a tight budget who can't afford to pay the extra three bucks.) Note: I've since learned that wood floors should usually be swept. Mopping can damage them. They should only be mopped with a damp sponge, using as little water as possible or with special cleaner for wood. It's OK to use a regular mop ans water on linoleum or tile.

The kitchen was looking so good that I was about to clean the cupboard and under the refrigerator. But that was too much right then, so I moved on to the next room.

Scrubbing the Bathroom

Remember those cats I told you about? Well, not only do they pee under the stove, they also think it is fun to rip down every shower curtain I buy. So part of cleaning the bathroom was putting up yet another shower curtain to keep water in the shower.

Scrub That Tub

Scrub the bath tub, toilet and sink regularly using an abrasive porcelain cleanser, like Ajax. The longer you don't clean your toilet or bath tub, the harder it becomes to make them sparkle!

After that, I used a wet sponge with Soft Scrub to wipe down the sink, my toothbrush holder, the tub and the toilet. Soft Scrub gets off the dirt and scum, but doesn't damage the tile or fixtures. Then I swept and mopped the floor with a mixture of half water, half bleach. I cleaned the toilet with a little Soft Scrub and a cleaning brush. Simple…except for the fact that the toilet seat broke apart and the cats kept jumping in the tub while I was cleaning it, leaving their dirty little paw prints all over. Eventually I had to just throw them in the closet. Now I know what you animal lovers are saying, I should have just closed the bathroom door, but once I put vinegar and bleach in the toilet and got some noxious fumes, so I clean with the door open. I've since learned <u>never</u> to combine bleach with an acid like vinegar, or especially ammonia. It can create a poisonous gas.

(You might be wondering how I can stand to live in an ol' stinky apartment with a bunch of nasty, pee-everywhere animals. Well, I'm lonely. That's how.)

www.youthcomm.org

Bleach Smells Away

Pew! Get rid of smells with bleach or another disinfectant, which kills germs. Mix bleach with water—about a cup of bleach to a quart of water— to wipe down kitchen counters and mop floors and to disinfect things that smell bad, like kitchen trash cans. But be careful—bleach can stain your clothes.

After cleaning the kitchen and bathroom, I went through the rest of the house. I straightened the closets and gave them a quick clean with the broom. Then I straightened, swept and wiped down the floor in my main room. (But just a note, I don't mop like normal people do. I scrub the floor first. I get on my hands and knees with a scrub brush and a bucket filled with hot water and dish soap and scrub a small area, I quickly wipe up the water and dirt from that area. Then I do the next spot. It might sound crazy, but I swear it's the only way to get those floors really clean.)

Finally, I went to what some people call my "foyer." I say to that, "Get real. It's called an entry hall." A pretty dirty entry hall, too. That's where I keep my CDs, and I came across one I hadn't heard in a while. Of course, I had to put it on to see if I still remembered the words.

Interruptions like this are why it can take me all day to clean my small studio apartment.

Caring for My Clothes Keeps Me Looking Good: Here's How I Do It

By KAREEM BANKS

Kareem Banks

I take my image seriously, because I think the better you look the better you feel. If you feel more confident, you might get more attention from the opposite sex or have an easier time on that job interview.

So I always try to dress to perfection. Knowing how to do laundry right plays a big part in this. All the brand name clothes in the world can look good the first time you wear them, but if you can't keep them clean they're not going to look good for long. So unless you make enough money to wear your clothes only once before you get rid of them, you better learn how to do your laundry.

Here's how I do mine:

1. Check the Tags for Washing Instructions.
Some might say "Dry Clean Only." These clothes are usually made of material like wool or silk that is too delicate to go through a washing machine. They are usually clothes like sweaters, windbreakers, and fitted hats. These clothes need to be taken to a dry cleaner (which can be expensive) or can sometimes be washed by hand, usually in cold water, using a gentle soap suitable for hand-washing, like Woolite, or even dishwashing liquid or shampoo.

2. Empty Your Pockets.
That way, you don't wash important things, like money, or a pen with ink that spills out and ruins your whole laundry.

3. Separate Clothes by Color.

Colors—this includes clothes that are dark-colored like red, black, blue and denim jeans. Colors usually get washed with cold water so that the colors don't fade or run. I usually turn my jeans inside out when washing them, because they fade less that way.

Lights—this includes clothes that are light, like white, tan or light yellow. Lights can get washed with warm water, but today's cold water detergents make that unnecessary, especially if you pay the gas or electric bill.

4. Put Each Pile of Clothing in a Separate Washing Machine. (Except for the hand-washables.)

If you're at a laundromat, put in the quarters you need to turn the machine on. Select the right temperature for the clothes you're washing. (Most machines have instructions for how to do this.) Then add detergent.

The only time you should use regular bleach is when washing only white clothes. If you spill bleach on colored clothes, your darkest clothes will turn white. (This should give you an idea of how strong the bleach is.)

Though this is the usual way to wash clothes, some people have their own method of how to wash, and as you become an expert at laundry you may come up with your own style. Some people use fabric softener, and I've even seen people put cologne and perfume in there. (I only use fragrances when I'm ironing the clean clothes to get out any wrinkles.)

5. Dry Clothes. You can put all colors that fit in the dryer together. But read the instructions on the clothes, because some clothes should be hung to dry or else they might shrink or get too wrinkled.

Personally, I don't dry clothes except for socks and drawers. I've found that the dryer usually shrinks my clothes too much and I like my clothes baggy. Instead, I hang dry my clothes by putting them on a hanger when they come out of the wash. Then I let the fan hit them or I hang them outside on a wire when it's windy and warm out.

Shirts can be difficult. You have to be careful because when they're wet, they're a bit heavy. So if you hang them the normal way on a hanger, the neckline might stretch from the weight and dry that way. If this happens, it's a wrap, because it won't go back to the normal size. This is bad if you wear wife-beaters (tank tops) under your shirts, because they'll show and this looks tacky. So fold your shirts evenly without any ripples in the fold, then put them out to dry that way.

6. Iron. Ironing clothes gets out their wrinkles, when you do it right. But it can be tricky to learn how to iron properly, so ask someone who knows to show you. If you fold your clothes carefully immediately out of the dryer you can eliminate the need for most ironing.

Remember: Keeping your clothes clean is like keeping them healthy. Just like people need food, exercise, and fresh air to stay healthy, clothes need regular cleaning and care to stay healthy, fresh and smelling good.

Activity Page for Group Leaders

Doing Laundry

Topic: Laundry

Goal: Help teens learn how to do laundry

Time: 1 hour and 25 minutes

What you'll need: Dirty laundry (a wool sweater from the Goodwill—that you can shrink in the dryer—is a good addition; laundry detergent; softener; bleach; stain remover; quarters; hangers; nearby laundromat

Discussion: 10 minutes

■ **Tell teens you're going to do laundry.** Focus on a few key issues: sorting light from dark, the value of washing some items inside out, like jeans and sweaters; cold vs. warm or hot wash; and the use of fabric softener and bleach.

Activity: 1 hour and 15 minutes

■ **Go to the Laundromat.**

■ **Sort laundry into darks and lights.**

■ **Have teens look at the care tags for anything that looks delicate or special, like clothes that require a cold wash or dry cleaning.**

■ **Have teens find stains and put stain remover on them.**

■ **Ask a teen to demonstrate how to load the washer.** Point out that if they stuff it to the brim the clothes will not clean as well and will be more wrinkled.

■ **Talk about bleach.** Nowadays, it's unnecessary for most clothes, but if you use it you have to be very careful not to ruin clothes with drips, etc. If you have dark clothes that can be thrown out, demonstrate what bleach does to them.

■ **When clothes are washed, have teens put them in the dryer.** Explain why you can now mix light and dark clothes, but, once again, don't cram it too full or drying will take too long. If you have a wool sweater that you can throw out, put it in the dryer to demonstrate how wool shrinks in heat.

■ **Have students hang items that cannot be dried on hangers.** Point out that they can save money by line drying items like blankets or jeans that take a long time to dry.

■ **When clothes are dry, have students remove them from the dryer.**

■ **Demonstrate how to fold basic items.**

Note: If possible, have the teens read Kareems' story on doing laundry (p. 171) while the clothes are washing and drying. Or, try to pick a laundromat with a TV so the teens will not get bored.

An Apology to All Group Home Cooks

By LENNY JONES

Through my four years in foster care, I have constantly ranted and raved about the things I don't like about the system. I have held a grudge

Lenny Jones

against things and people who have pissed me off, and I am here to say that I am sorry.

I am not sorry for everything I have said, but one of the things I am sorry about is the anger that I have taken out on all the group home cooks who have tried to poison (oh, I'm sorry, I meant nourish) me with food (usually pre-cooked and frozen) that they slaved over a hot microwave to prepare, just so I could have something lukewarm (which I usually threw in the trash when they weren't looking) to come home to.

I Can't Cook!

I am giving this sincere apology because now the tables have turned on me. I have moved into my agency's apartment program (they give me and another resident our own apartment so we can learn how to live on our own) and have come to a startling conclusion: I can't cook!!!

> **The chicken was already cut into parts, so I tossed in the first victim (a wing) and in a few seconds it turned black!**

Well, let me take that back...I can make a mean bowl of cereal, but that is about it. I have tried cooking before, but I nearly poisoned myself a few times. I even had step-by-step instructions, but I still messed up.

For instance, a friend gave me directions on how to fry chicken. First, she said I had to defrost it. But since I didn't have a microwave, it would take a few hours.

How Do You Clean a Chicken?

So to shorten the time, I put the pieces in a pot of scalding hot water for about 15 minutes. Well, the chicken itself didn't defrost, but the skin cooked, and it ended up at the bottom of the pot.

Then my friend told me to clean the chicken with water and lemon juice.

Now me being the cooking idiot that I am, I figured that you clean a chicken like you clean yourself, with soap and hot water. And why should I use a lemon when I had Lemon Fresh Dawn?

I figured I was way ahead of the game (big mistake).

So now, here I am, sudsing up the poor chicken's wings and legs, thinking how good it smells and how great it's going to taste.

Next, she told me to grease the pan. After I greased it, I turned the flame on as high as it could go. I don't know whether you've ever experienced this joyful celebration of grease, fireworks, and loud popping, but once you have, it's something you'll never forget (or recover from).

I got popped right between the eyes and it hurt like a "bleep."

The chicken was already cut into parts, so I tossed in the first victim (a wing) and in a few seconds it turned black!

Then I realized that I forgot the batter. So I grabbed a bag of corn meal (don't ask) and battered them.

Then I turned down the flame. I put a few pieces in and watched them cook. (At least that is what I thought they were doing.)

Suddenly, I saw these weird looking suds that smelled a lot like lemon. I knew that something wasn't right when the dough started rising and crumbling off.

I called my friend up to ask what I did wrong. When I told her what I did, she busted out laughing and told me to throw it out and order Chinese.

That night I ate takeout. But since then I've had more kitchen disasters.

The first time I tried to make Carolina rice, I followed the instructions on the bag, but things still didn't work out as planned.

The instructions said for every cup of rice, I should use two cups of water. So I poured the rice into my measuring cup and thought to myself, "This isn't enough for me to eat," not realizing that rice expands when it cooks.

So I put in three cups of rice (another one of my classic bad ideas) and six cups of water. If I had been able to cook it, I probably would have had enough rice for an entire week.

But I wasn't. Somehow I wound up with all this excess water.

The package said to let it simmer, but I must have been simmering that rice for about an hour. By the time it finished, the rice was all sticky and clumpy.

I threw it out and started over. This time I used one cup of rice and two cups of water, but I ended up with the same problem.

So I got smart (or at least I thought I did) and used paper towels. Of course you know that came out a disaster! The tissue was falling apart in the rice and it was just horrible.

Burnt and Crunchy

I tried one last time that same night. I used one cup of rice and one and a half cups of water. I came so close, I tell you. The only thing was that the rice ended up half-cooked and burnt at the bottom.

At least now I've found a foolproof way of making rice. Uncle Ben's has "Rice in a Bag." You just put the bag in boiling water for 10 minutes, and it comes out perfect every time.

Not every one of my cooking attempts has been a disaster. I've mastered one thing: salmon! All I need is an onion, Pam cooking spray, and seasoning salt. I just sauté the chopped onions, throw in the salmon, and add the seasoning (no biggie).

Wash Meaty Messes

Meat that's not cooked may contain bacteria that can make you sick. When you're cooking meat, use warm, soapy water to wash everywhere that uncooked meat has touched, including counters, cutting boards, knives and dishes.

www.youthcomm.org

But after eating salmon for two weeks in a row, I got sick of it.

Lots of Cold Cereal

I can also make turkey burgers and a few other things. But my diet largely consists of takeout (which leaves me crying broke)! When I can't afford Chinese or pizza, I live on cold cereal, canned foods and junk.

It's times like these that make me wish I had someone to cook for me. Even though I've exaggerated the monstrosities that the group home cooks invented every day (i.e. marinated monkey hips with rice and curried rat), I really miss them.

If I could turn back the clock, I would have spent every moment I could in the kitchen with the cooks, learning every bit I could.

I guess that would be my one bit of advice to you—be observant and ask whoever is cooking if you can help out in making dinner for the house. Soon you'll be on your own, and besides worrying about a roof over your head, you'll also need a hot meal in your stomach.

Cookbooks Help Me Survive

Another thing that is helping me survive on my own is cookbooks, like the Complete Idiot's Guide to Cooking, the Five in Ten Cookbook (five ingredients in ten minutes), and the Six Ingredients or Less Cookbook. From these books, I've learned how to make all kinds of quick and easy things, like salmon cakes, chicken cutlet parmesan, different types of pastas, and sandwiches. Most of them come out burnt or half-cooked, but I'm still trying.

Cookbooks aren't as good as having someone teach you, but at least they're a start.

So for those who have the luxury of learning from someone who can cook (even a group home cook), take advantage of it every chance you get. Or else, you may soon wind up like me—living on Frosted Flakes.

Rinse Your Fruit

An apple a day keeps the doctor away... unless it's covered with pesticides. Pesticides are chemicals farmers spray on fruits and vegetables to keep bugs away. To get rid of them, thoroughly rinse fruits and vegetables with water before you cook or eat them.

www.youthcomm.org

Help Yourself:
How to Eat Healthy

By NATASHA SANTOS

Teens are not known for eating well. In fact, we're notorious for supersizing fast food. But we can improve our eating habits and our health by taking just a few tiny steps. I learned this when I took a workshop on healthy eating. Here are some suggestions for eating healthy.

Natasha Santos

1. Eat at Least Three Times a Day.

That means reasonable portions of nutritious foods such as fruits, vegetables, chicken, turkey, fish, and whole grains at least three times a day. Skipping meals won't help you lose weight or concentrate. (A "meal" does not mean nachos, Twix bars, or anything containing man-manufactured sweeteners or hydrogenated oils—basically anything that sounds like it can burn a hole through your stomach.)

2. Know Your Limits. If you drink a lot of soda or eat a bunch of candy, you'll get hyper and then really tired. Limit the junk you eat so you'll feel energetic all day.

3. Read Labels! Manufacturers are required to list ingredients and nutritional information on containers to let you know how much—or how little—nutrition is inside. Nutrition facts give you a general idea of the fats, calories and nutrients in foods. You want to eat foods with lots of vitamins and fiber, and avoid fats and sugars.

4. Snack on Fruit, Vegetables, or Pretzels

instead of chips, chocolate, or candy. This takes some getting used to, but it pays off. The less sugar you eat, the sweeter fruit will taste.

5. Avoid Fried Foods. Fast food and greasy foods like fried chicken and French fries are OK only once in a while—and in small

portions. When you're cooking, remember that olive, canola and vegetable oils are much better for you than butter, lard or margarine.

6. Drink Eight Glasses of Water Each Day.
Water cleans out your body, and it fills you up so you don't eat too much. Sometimes when you think you're hungry, you're just thirsty. Water is a lot better for you than juice or soda.

7. Know Your Body Type. Don't starve yourself for any
reason—for attention, to prove you're in control, or to get a "perfect" body. Accept and celebrate what you've got.

8. Indulge Occasionally. Everyone needs a taste of
Haagen Dazs or a cherry cheese danish once in a while. But if this becomes habit you need to re-evaluate your eating habits and get back on a healthy track.

9. Only Eat When You're Hungry. Don't eat to feel
calm, comforted, happy, or loved. If you're eating to soothe your emotions, find activities to help improve your mood (a hot bath, a good book, exercise, dance, writing in a diary). Some people find that therapy helps them to understand why they eat when they don't really need to.

My Recipes

Next time your grandma or your foster mom makes your favorite mac and cheese, or your boyfriend cooks you a romantic spaghetti dinner, get the recipe! Use these next few pages to record your favorite recipes so you'll have them when you're in your own. (And won't go bankrupt on takeout!)

My Recipes

My Recipes

Activity Page for Group Leaders

How to Keep House on a Budget

Topic: Who can come up with the cheapest list of cleaning materials for a new apartment?

Goal: To help teens recognize the key cleaning chores involved in living on their own. To help teens become smart consumers of cleaning supplies.

Time: 1 hour and 15 minutes

Activity: The Cheap Cleaning Challenge

■ **Tell students** to imagine that they're moving into a new apartment and they have to buy a month's worth of cleaning supplies. Their goal is to spend as little as possible while still getting the items they need. (You can have students do this exercise individually or in teams.)

■ **Lay down the rules:** They have to "buy" items to clean dishes, the sink, countertops, kitchen floor (probably linoleum), other floors (assume they are wood, not carpeted), toilet, and glass.

You can decide how much guidance you want to give (maybe not much so that you'll get a wide range of costs from the kids).

■ **Send the teens to a local store.** Give them the list on p. 185 which has: Item Name, Size, Cost, and Purpose for each thing they would buy. (For example, Ivory Liquid, 12 oz., $3, for cleaning dishes.) They must complete all four columns for

each item they would buy. Then they should add up each item for a total cost.

Tips: Here are some typical and not so typical ways that students can save money. See which of these they do, and praise the kids who do them. (One important aspect of this lesson is to show the kids they already know a lot about how to save money. Another is to share strategies.) If they don't think of some of these things, tell them (at the end of the discussion).

1) Buy the generic brand instead of a brand name.

2) Buy an appropriate size (not so large you'll never use it all; not so small that you're paying a lot per ounce)

3) Substitute: If you have a small apartment, do you really need a mop? An old t-shirt and a little elbow grease can keep your floors sparkling. You don't really need Windex; you can clean glass with ammonia and water. Do you really need a roll of paper towels? A dishrag and a hand washing rag might be enough. Do you really need Tidy Bowl when a small sprinkle of the Ajax you use to clean the sink will do just fine in the toilet?

The winner is the teen who gets all the items he or she needs to clean the apartment at the lowest cost. When you're done, ask the teens if they can see a way to beat even the lowest cost now that they've seen each teen's strategy.

ITEM NAME	SIZE	COST	PURPOSE
	TOTAL		

Test Yourself:
How Clean is Your Crib?

1. Putting a wool sweater in the dryer will:

a) Make the rest of your clothes smell like the lamb the wool came from.

b) Cause the dryer and possibly Laundromat to burst into flames. Wool combusts under heat.

c) Make a new sweater for your baby sister! Wool shrinks in the dryer.

2. Spilling bleach directly on your jeans will:

a) Give them that fresh, clean smell you can't get enough of.

b) Give you an excuse to ask for help from the cute girl or guy at the laundry machine next to you. The bright white, permanent spot the bleach makes will make it clear you need help.

c) Turn your skin alarmingly white next time you manage to fit into them.

3. You know it's time to wash the sheets on your bed when:

a) It's your birthday. Once a year is about right!

b) It's time to buy a new set—the sheets start looking holier than swiss cheese. (And I don't mean in the Biblical sense!)

c) You go to the laundromat—about once every 2-3 weeks.

4. When buying cleaning supplies, buying the generic (or store) brand will:

a) Mean you'll never get your house to sparkle like you can with the brand name product.

b) Save you mega money and wow visitors with how smart you are. Generic is the same as the brand name, only cheaper.

c) Create a health hazard—who knows what the heck they put in those products?

5. Before you mop any floors without carpet, it's a good idea to:

a) Pray for rain and a leaky ceiling. Then maybe you won't have to mop after all.

b) Take a few laps around the place on something with wheels since it will be too slippery for that when the floor is drying—skateboards, rollerblades, or motor bikes will do.

c) Sweep first, so you're not creating a muddy mess.

Turn page to see the correct answers.

Answers:
How Clean is Your Crib?

1. Putting a wool sweater in the dryer will:

c) Make a new sweater for your baby sister! Wool shrinks in the dryer.

2. Spilling bleach directly on your jeans will:

b) Give you an excuse to ask for help from the cute girl or guy at the laundry machine next to you. The bright white, permanent spot the bleach makes will make it clear you need help.

3. You know it's time to wash the sheets on your bed when:

c) You go to the laundromat about once every 1-2 weeks. After all, you change those once a day but you lie in your bed every night.

4. When buying cleaning supplies, buying the generic (or store) brand will:

b) Save you mega money and wow visitors with how smart you are. Generic is the same as the brand name, only cheaper.

5. Before you mop any floors without carpet, it's a good idea to:

c) Sweep first. That way you won't mop the dirt into the ground.

www.youthcomm.org

Chapter 7

Mysteries and Miseries—
Love, Sex, and Relationships

Mysteries and Miseries: Why This Chapter Matters

I grew up in a home where love was shown through sex, so it was natural for me to think I could find love through sex. I slept with quite a lot of men while I was living in a group home. Having men want me made me feel beautiful and erased my sadness. I always felt better when they were holding me.

Ijeoma Okolo

In my heart, I really didn't want to sleep with them, but I thought if I didn't, I would lose them. I was too scared of being lonely and rejected to say "no."

Last year, when I moved out of foster care and into my own apartment, my loneliness hit me harder than ever. Being on my own was such a shock that I started to realize that I had to deal with my problems, not escape them with drink and sex. I decided that I needed to be more in control.

So I made a decision to drink less and not sleep with men I really didn't know, and for now, I've stopped. But that doesn't mean that I don't have the desire to do them even now. I do, because I never dealt with the pain that brought me into the system.

Like me, a lot of teens in care carry pain from their pasts and being separated from their families. This pain can affect their feelings about love and sex. Some like me confuse sex with security. Some of us want to be close to someone so badly we'll put up with just about anything. Some of us are afraid of getting hurt and give too little. Of course, all teens struggle with these same things, but these emotions can feel especially intense for those of us who have had to grow up without family.

This chapter is about sex and love relationships. We explore how our pasts affected our attitudes toward love and sex, and our struggles to find love and companionship in ways that work best for us.

We hope our stories help you explore how your own upbringing has shaped you. We also hope they'll help you figure out what you want from a love relationship, what you hope to be able to give, and how to continue taking care of yourself when you're in love.

—Ijeoma Okolo

What Does It Mean to Respect Yourself on a Date?

Wait for the females to go in first.

—**Kenny G., 16**
Linden Center School
Los Angeles, Calif.

The opportunity to be with that person and learn more about him or her and do it through having fun.

—**Johnnesha W., 16**
United Care
Los Angeles, Calif.

Don't let the boy touch you. A hug would be OK, but feeling on your thigh would go too far. A kiss on the cheek is appropriate, but no tongue.

—**Naia L., 16**
United Care
Los Angeles, Calif.

Learning to Love Again

By SHANIQUA SOCKWELL

As a child, I always saw love as a magical force that could draw two people together forever. I read about love in fairy tales, saw it in movies and heard it on the radio. But I never experienced it in real life.

I would watch men and women holding hands, kissing and looking into each other's eyes, sharing special messages that only they could understand. I would wonder, "Why can't I have that? Just once I'd like to have someone tell me they love me and really mean it."

Like Isn't Love

After a while, I started dating. I soon wished I hadn't.

Instead of taking things slow, I would instantly get caught up in the guy. Looking back, I realize I mistook like for love, so it's no wonder I got hurt many times. Lord knows I've had my share of heartache from men who used this word to control me. They all knew my weakness: that I was in great need. From that, they drew their ability to hurt me.

One boyfriend would tell me he cared for me, and I almost believed him. But if he cared, why did he sleep with my cousin when I wouldn't give it up?

Another boyfriend said that he liked me a lot, that I was funny and sweet, and I wasn't like other girls. But is liking me not telling me that he was cheating on me?

One guy who told me he loved me said I reminded him of his mother. How sweet, but does being in love with me mean telling my mother that you're breaking up with me before you tell me?

No Decent Men

Only a fool would put up with this for as long as I did. I began to dislike men with a passion. I stopped dating because I felt that I had been hurt enough. Besides, being alone was far better than being with someone who made me feel bad.

It seemed that I couldn't find a decent man. But on the other hand, I didn't want to believe that all men are dogs because I know not all of them are. So what was I supposed to think?

I began to wonder why I was in need of love so much, why I was so dependent on having someone to call my own. That was when I realized that I never had someone in my childhood to show me any kind of affection, which is why I didn't really know what the word love meant. I mean, I knew what it meant, but I didn't know how to express it, give it or receive it because I didn't receive it as a child.

My biological mother always had a funny way of showing how much she loved me. The closest kind of affection I ever got from her was, "Yeah, I love your dumb ass, now go do the dishes!!" She didn't know what kind of effect this had on me, even when I did the dishes with tears coursing down my cheeks.

> **Love is a strong word. Lord knows I've had my fair share of heartache from men who used this word to control me.**

Some people say, "The first man you ever fall in love with is your father." What if all you had was a "daddy" who did drugs and came in all hours of the night and went around with a bunch of different women who you could never imagine calling "Mom"? Would you love "Daddy" then? My daddy told me he loved me all the time, but, like Mom, he had a funny way of showing it. By looking at how my parents treated me as a child, I realized I had to love myself and accept myself.

I'd always felt bad about myself. Basically, I was looking for a loving relationship to replace that missing self-esteem. But I had to realize that another person doesn't give you that self-esteem. You have to feel it inside yourself before you enter a serious relationship.

Looking for a Fantasy

Through talking things out with people and thinking about my past relationships, I discovered exactly what my problem was. I was looking for love not in the wrong places, but in the wrong way.

I was searching for my Nubian prince, my knight in shining armor, but I was attracted to fantasy figures because I didn't have a successful male figure in my childhood. I had no idea of what kind of person I should be attracted to.

My Needs First

Instead of looking for a fantasy, I started to put my needs first. For example, one of my ex's used to stand me up on dates. I couldn't deal with it, but I'd let it slide because I really liked him. Then I realized that I was ignoring my own feelings. So I looked for someone who wouldn't stand me up.

Today, I am much happier. I have a man who loves me as much as I love him. We see each other often. We write love letters. We talk. And even more important, he realizes that I have a working brain and that I use it.

But even though I love him, my senses are keen and aware that the relationship could end at any time. Maybe it comes from being hurt so much and developing a distrust of men. I don't want to be the one working overtime to keep the relationship going, never getting any credit, and then be left holding the pink slip.

But time has a way of healing old wounds, and I've learned to be comfortable with myself, whether I'm in a love relationship or not.

And although I haven't come completely full circle when it comes to how I think about myself, I can now say that I love myself a lot more than I did a few years ago.

Love Doesn't Have to Hurt...
How to stay cool when a relationship gets hot

By DELICIA JONES

When I broke up with Kevin, I felt like life was over. I kept remembering the way we used to talk about whatever was going on in the world. I remembered him taking me shopping and telling me what he wanted to see me wearing. All I could do was replay scenes from our relationship, trying to figure out how we went from being in love to not wanting to be in the same room with each other.

It took me three long months to get over Kevin. During that time I felt so bad. I thought that I would never love anyone like I loved Kevin.

The pain that I felt from breaking up with Kevin made me realize that you can't base your life on just one person, no matter how strongly you feel about him or her. That can only hurt you in the long run.

Once I did finally get over Kevin, I was determined to never again be so upset about a breakup. I decided that I wouldn't let my world center around one guy again. I wanted to learn how to be in a relationship and still have other important things in my life—like fun with my female friends, like time to myself. So I came up with ways to have a healthy relationship and avoid too much heartache if it does end.

Now don't get me wrong. I'm not telling you it's not good to love, because I don't think that. All I'm saying is, don't get so wrapped up in that one person that you don't have anything else going on in your life and you don't have anyone or anything to fall back on if it ends. Here's how.

Rule #1: Never Put Your Friends Last.

No matter what your boo tells you, friends were there before he or she got in your life, and if they're truly your friends, they'll be there after he or she leaves. Friends should be people you can really count on, so (if you want to keep them) treat them well, even when you're in a relationship.

Once I put my boyfriend before my friends. I would always tell my friends things like, "I can't go out with you because I have a date with my boyfriend," knowing that my boyfriend had only asked me to go somewhere five minutes earlier.

After a couple of times of doing that, my friends decided that I wasn't really being a good friend and that they didn't have time for me and my excuses. They started to leave me out of things and stopped calling me.

Well, as you already know, me and that guy broke up. Guess who I turned to? That's right, my old friends. They were kind of upset with me, but I was lucky. They forgave me. Still, I learned never to do that again.

Rule #2: Don't Get Too Hooked on Your New Love.

Don't make your schedule revolve around everything that person does. Make some time just to be alone to reflect on your relationship and to get better acquainted with yourself. You might like to take yourself shopping or rent some movies and just relax.

I can remember a time when all I did was what Kevin wanted to do. I was watching baseball and soccer with him no matter how tired I was. After a while I began to notice that I wasn't doing the girlie things I liked to do, like going to see those movies that you know will make you cry, or talking on the phone with my girlfriends. I was starting to feel I had no say in my own life. I was only doing what made Kevin happy.

Now I make sure to let my new boyfriend know what I want to do. I tell him that there are certain things I won't watch on TV just because I don't want to. I also make time to do things by myself. Even though I'm dating someone, I still feel like I'm running my own life.

Rule #3: Don't Use Those Three Famous Words, "I Love You."

Or at least don't use them in the early stages of a relationship. Those words can complicate any relationship, especially if they're used too early. They can make a relationship hard, because saying you love a person means a lot to some people.

These words can make the other person too open. He or she might begin to feel too intensely about you too soon. He or she might think nothing will ever break you up, even if you're not actually feeling that way. So to avoid hurting others and getting hurt, use those words carefully.

This one boy I was dealing with always used to say he loved me. Most of the time I just said, "Thank you," or "OK." One day he got sick of hearing just that from me, and he asked me to say "I love you" back.

Being an open and honest person, I told him that I wouldn't because I really didn't love him. By the expression on his face, I could see that those words hurt him. Then he didn't call me for about three weeks. I finally got up enough courage to call him and ask if he wanted to do something. He said he didn't have time.

As you probably guessed, we didn't last long after that. But I don't regret what I said because I didn't love him and I didn't want to mislead him.

Still, I wish I could have changed the wording. Maybe it wouldn't have hurt him so much.

So here's a way to let your mate down without hurting him or her completely. If he or she asks you to say those words and you don't feel like it's time or you feel like you're not in love, simply put it like this: "I don't want to say those words yet because I'm still getting to know you and I'm still learning more about you." You might learn to love that person!

> **Don't get so wrapped up in that one person that you don't have anyone or anything to fall back on if it does end.**

What You Can Do

Enough about what you shouldn't do. Here are some of the things that you can do to show that you do depend on your mate without needing them to hold your world together.

Send your boo little gifts to show that he or she is on your mind. You can call every day to let him or her know they still come first. You can talk about your day, your job, what you were thinking about doing, or anything that might have crossed your mind.

These are the things good relationships are made of—saying sweet things and doing sweet things for each other and talking a lot. So don't try to start a relationship with someone you feel you can't talk to or couldn't be friends with.

If you're just looking for someone to play around with, then you can pick that person with your eyes closed. But if you're looking for someone you want to have a relationship with, you have a lot of thinking to do.

Taking My Own Advice

If you can't hold a mature conversation with this person without it resulting in an argument or without it becoming something immature, he or she is not a potential friend and shouldn't be a potential mate.

In my current relationship, I try to listen to my own advice and it's hard. There are times when my boyfriend will say, "Let's go see a movie," and I already have plans to go roller-skating with my friends. Lots of times I'd rather go out with my boyfriend, but I remember my advice and tell him, "I already have plans for tonight, but if you can hold that thought until tomorrow, we can do it then."

Now that I'm following my own advice, I'm having fun with my boyfriend and feeling good about myself.

What Do You Consider a Date?

"When someone asks you out. I think whoever asks the person out should pay."

—Lisa M., 17
United Care
Los Angeles, Calif.

"Anything two people can do that they both enjoy."

—Zack W., 16
Linden Center School
Los Angeles, Calif.

"When the couple goes out and has a great time."

—Karina O., 15
Linden Center School
Los Angeles, Calif.

"When a guy takes you out on a nice
date without asking you to pay for it, and he volunteers
to get you a doggy bag. He doesn't bring his friend along
or his mother. His cell phone is off."

—Naia L., 16
United Care
Los Angeles, Calif.

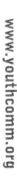

www.youthcomm.org

What are grounds for breaking up?

"When you stop respecting each other or when you feel yourself growing apart."

—Johnnesha W., 16
United Care
Los Angeles, Calif.

"When somebody cheats on somebody or you're just not feeling them no more. Or first you thought their personality was cool but then it was all ugly."

—Nakeya M., 17
United Care
Los Angeles, Calif.

"If he cheats on you, if he spreads rumors about you or you don't feel comfortable around him."

—Lisa M., 17
United Care
Los Angeles, Calif.

"When a guy decides to choose his friends over you. When he disrespects you. When he cheats or when he decides to act a fool and put up a front in front of his friends and family members."

—Naia L., 16
United Care
Los Angeles, Calif.

When Sex Is Easy and Love Is Hard

I was trained to please everyone but myself.

By CHRISTINE McKENNA

I like to think I've changed, that I'm not the same person I was years ago, and I guess I have. I suppose the tell-tale sign of change is when you

Christine McKenna

look back at yourself and all the things you've done and either cringe in disbelief or feel nothing at all. I cringe. Boy, do I ever! This was me then:

I was a b-tch. Really a not-nice-person. Fighting, drugs, alcohol. And then there were the men. A lot of men. I had this ability to find the most messed up people in the world and attach myself to them.

Sexually Abused as a Toddler

I was promiscuous. To put it bluntly, I was a slut. I had no qualms about hooking up with guys. The older the better. A lot of people might say this was because I was abused since I was 2 by my father and a bunch of other guys my mother brought into the house. And that was part of it—I learned early that sex was something I was good at, something that people wanted and that I could give them.

I lost my virginity (not technically 'cause of the whole dad thing, but I say that's when I lost it cause this counts and that didn't) when I was 11. I was best friends with this guy named Newton. Newton was cute and cool and just a little bit dangerous. He was also 14—old compared to my 11. My mom couldn't stand him which made him all the more desirable.

I Pushed Sex On My Best Friend

Newton and I were friends for a few months, and nothing happened between us sexually. Not for my lack of trying though. I wanted him to have sex with me. I wanted to see how sex felt with someone other than my father. I heard people saying how great it was.

But Newton wouldn't do it. He said he liked me as a friend and didn't want to ruin that. Plus, I was too young. This did not make sense to me. I could not believe a guy would want only friendship with a girl. If he liked the girl at all, wouldn't he want to sleep with her? So I decided the problem was me: What was I doing wrong to make him not want me?

I tried harder. I started skipping school and inviting him over to watch movies and "hang out." One day he brought over some porn and we smoked a little weed and I saw that the tape was turning him on. Now was my chance. He responded. We had sex.

And oddly, that bothered me.

Though at first I couldn't deal with the fact that Newton didn't want to have sex with me, now that he did want to I hated it. I hated that all his concerns about me being too young or how he liked being my friend left his mind the minute he got excited. It only fueled my belief that all men will do anything, even what they think is "wrong," once they become horny.

> **It's all a blur of Absolut vodka and Purple Haze and back seats and alleyways. Then the high ended and I was depressed as hell and all alone.**

And then I wasn't thrilled with the sex. What the hell was I was expecting? Maybe I was doing it all wrong or maybe I was just 11. Whatever the case, I just got scared during it. I remember lying there thinking, "God, when will this be over?"

Messing Up and Messing Around

When I was 14, I came into foster care, which was hell for me. I hated the caged feeling of being in a lock down. I wasn't supposed to do anything. No smoking, no drinking, no sex. I had all this time now to focus on me and I really didn't like what I was.

I was an emotional wreck, but I didn't want to deal with this piece of me. I liked numbing out. Trouble helped me numb out. So I looked for trouble.

In group homes, I kept messing up and messing around: AWOLing every night to the brewery next door. Smoking in the building. Making out with guys in plain view of the staff. It didn't matter that most of the time I felt terrible and that every time I slept with a guy I felt like putting a bullet in my brain. This was supposed to be fun dammit. Every one of my friends said so. This was living. The time of my life.

Proud of My Skills

After I emancipated from foster care and moved to Santa Monica, a beach town where I lived in the YWCA, and where there's surf and turf and enough weed to get a contact high from walking down the street, I felt that I should take full advantage of my freedom even if it killed me.

I can't even recall all the stuff I did in that time right after I left the system. It's all a blur of Absolut Vodka and Purple Haze and back seats and alleyways. Then the high ended and I was depressed as hell and all alone. I suddenly realized I was merely surviving from day to day, not living. And I started to admit to myself that though I was having a lot of sex, I really didn't like it.

Oh, I liked everything that led up to sex. I liked how it felt when I spotted the guy, flirted with the guy, teased the guy. It's a kind of dance, and I was good at it, and proud that I was good at it. But somehow I was always surprised when it turned from "hey shorty" to "suck my dick, b-tch."

But why was I surprised? What was I expecting anyway, after all I'd seen and done? Romeo or something? Someone who would look beyond my defenses and notice the scared little girl I was? Someone who actually cared?

Still, I kept hooking up with men. I was stuck in pleasure mode, but it was their pleasure, not mine, that I cared about. I still don't know why I cared about pleasing them so damn much. Maybe I was just lonely. Maybe sex was the only way I knew how to connect with someone. Maybe I just wanted to prove that I was good at something. And sometimes it did feel good in the moment, even if it felt like hell afterward.

Afraid to Be Close

Oh I talked about how I liked sex and hated to be attached to some guy, but it wasn't true. What was true was that being close to someone— really close, the kind of closeness that involves kindness and tenderness and that you see on TV—terrified me.

Closeness leaves you vulnerable to all kinds of stuff that should be avoided, like having your heart stomped on or having someone throw your feelings in your face so you feel horrible. And as much as I needed connection with people, I didn't want them hurting me, so it made sense to hook up with guys who even I thought were jerks, because there was no chance I'd expect too much from them. You can bet I always made sure to do the leaving before I was left.

Couldn't Handle More than Sex

Then the game changed. I moved into a home for adults with mental disabilities and I was required to go to therapy. Here's my therapist: "How does that make you feel?…Talk about your feelings, not your actions," or my favorite, "Therapy is about me helping you find the answers, not me giving them to you."

I wasn't ready for that. I stayed pretty quiet in sessions. Meanwhile, I started noticing that though the men in my building may be crazy, they sure were cute! One of them even got attached to me. He wanted it all the time. I was pleased that he wanted me, but disgusted as well. Then he started getting all relationshippy with me. He wanted more from me than just sex, and I could not handle it. I decided to let him know that I could be with whomever I pleased whether he liked it or not.

Cut to me becoming the biggest slut in the building. Everyone in the building knew I was giving it away. Those months were a blur for me. I didn't want to even think about what I was doing to myself. It was easier to wake up in a strange bed with a strange guy and numb out than to deal with the fact that this was what I had reduced myself to.

A Therapist I Liked

After seeing three therapists, none who were very helpful to me, I started seeing a new therapist named Susan. I didn't think much about her at first. Just someone else to tell me what was wrong with me (which I already knew) but not to help me get better. But Susan was strange. I found myself actually talking to her, though most of the time only to argue. I love arguing with people, making them so mad that they forget they're there to help me. But with Susan it didn't work. She never fought back. I even told her I hated her and didn't want to talk to her, and she was all, "Well, then why do you keep talking to me?"

Hmm, good question.

I guess I liked talking to her. She let me vent and curse and talk about how messed up I was, without judging me. And the truth is I really am a pretty complicated person. I was—still am—a jumble of contradictions. I hate sex, but I feel a compulsion to it. I hate when men only want to sleep with me, but I can't take it when a man says he only wants to be friends. I want closeness but I hate to be touched. I want friends but I am mean to everyone who tries to get close to me. Yup, I'm all kinds of confused.

Making Better Choices

I don't want to say that Susan was the one thing that helped me to change, because she wasn't. I guess after I left care all these pieces started to come together, or fall apart rather, and she was there to help me pick up the pieces and see which ones I needed and which ones I could throw away.

I still can't explain all the contradictions of me, but I'm starting to understand myself better. That's helping me make some better choices, or at least understand why I make bad ones. I'm not saying I'm an angel, but I think a little more about the things I do, and that holds me a little more accountable for when I'm hurting myself.

But still the hardest thing for me to try to control, and even understand, is the sex thing.

I think my father messed me up more than I want to admit.

I hear people always talking about "making love," touching and kissing and feeling something other than them going up and down on you. I want to see what this is about. But letting myself get that close to someone, to let my defenses down that much, scares me. I don't feel I can ever trust a man that much.

Close Without Sex

Then a month ago I met this guy. Just a guy, nothing especially special about him, but he got to me. The closer I got to him, the farther away I wanted to run. He was making me feel all these things that I had never felt for anyone before. And the really funny thing is that I was scared of him! Me! Scared! Because he got me. I felt like he understood me. All my insecurities and confusing thought processes, and still he talked to me. And that's another thing. He didn't want to do anything with me sexually. He liked just talking to me. He found me interesting, and that made me feel like my words were worthy enough to be heard.

No man had ever made me feel like that. All the talking I had ever done with men before was sexual, or small talk before the sex started.

Part of me just wants to sleep with him and get it over with. Or maybe I should say "make love," which makes me want to laugh out loud—I never thought I would feel like doing that with any man, but with him it does seem like a possibility. But I worry that once we did that I would just hate him as much as I hate the other guys I've slept with, and I don't want that to happen.

It's so weird to be close to someone and not have sex with them. Sometimes we sit on the couch with my head on his shoulder and watch TV. Nothing happens, and not for my not wanting it to, but because he wants to be close to me without the sex. Sometimes, when we're on the couch in that position, I think he's making a move on me, wanting me to "perform" in some way. But he doesn't.

Before this, I've never been intimate with someone and not slept with him. It's a strange, new feeling, but it's also good. It makes me feel special, like maybe I'm more than just an easy lay. It's like he can see this person inside of me that I can't. Sometimes I find myself smiling just thinking of him.

'Do You Love Yourself?'

One night we were talking, and he asked me if I loved myself. I couldn't say I did, but out of nowhere this came out of my mouth: "I love the person I'm trying to become." It sounded like nonsense to me, but he thought that was very profound, and that made me think seriously about who I want to be.

I want to be the type of woman who doesn't see lust in every man's eyes. I want to be the type of woman who can hear "You look beautiful" without thinking of it as a sexual advance. I want to feel worthy of hugs that are soft and warm, of kisses that are sweet and lingering, of being in someone's arms and feeling it's OK to fall asleep. Maybe I'll never be that person. How can I know what the future holds? But then again maybe someday I will be that person I feel I could love.

We're Like Family

Nina and I have only been dating for five months, but in that short time we've gotten real tight. It's strange how sometimes we even seem to know what the other one is thinking. Like if we think about calling each other on the phone, or even something so simple as asking each other for a drink of water, we find it's already being done.

Maybe one of the reasons that we're so tight is that we don't have too many other people to rely on. We both had our biological parents die when we were younger. Very few of her other family members are still alive, and mine I'm not too close to. Nina and I try to fill in what's missing in each other's lives and become each other's family.

You can see this in the way Nina and I tend to baby and take care of each other, kind of like a parent would for a child. For example, if my hair were nappy, she would comb it for me. If I was cold, she would go to her house to get me one of her sweaters. When I was weak and sick, she kissed me so gently that it made me reminisce about places I've never been, like imagining the smell of Brazil.

And sometimes she turns to me like family, too. There was a time when I was weak from a head injury, but I still took her all the way home to make sure she had a safe and comfortable journey. Or when I have a weekend pass, she comes over and I make breakfast for her, like a regular couple.

It feels good when you have someone to lean on, especially if you've spent most of your life relying on yourself. If your relationship doesn't make it, you still always have you. But it's nice to have someone there, that special person, who can hold you down when you need it, and even when you don't.

—Oumar Bowman

Not Ready!

She was pregnant. I freaked.

By ANONYMOUS

(All names have been changed.)

One day in June, I received a phone call from a female acquaintance. We were conversating normally until she came out of nowhere and said, "I'm pregnant and I think it's yours." My eyes opened wide, and I asked her when this happened. "Remember back on October 2?" she said. "We did something."

I was stunned as I remembered what she was talking about. Then I couldn't think too well because anger came over me. I asked in a loud tone of voice, "How long did you know this? How many months are you?"

She told me that the baby was due next week and I was the father. I was furious. She had known this for nine months and was telling me only a week before the baby was due. I hung up on her.

Drunk at a Party

I sat there trying to get my thoughts together. I knew the time she was talking about. In October, I was chilling and getting drunk at a party and I saw her across the room. I approached her and asked how she was doing. She said, "I've been eyeing you all night, and was waiting for you to come to me."

I was amazed. I thought, "Oh really? Damn. That means I don't have to do that much." We went upstairs where the music wasn't so loud so we could talk alone. She told me that her name was Melanie and she didn't have a man but she was looking for one.

I said I was looking for someone too. That was a lie. Really I did have a woman, but I figured what she don't know won't hurt her.

Melanie started telling me about her life. She said her moms was a pain in the behind. She had an older brother who didn't care too much about her. I was kind of interested in her little tale. She said, "Let me get

www.youthcomm.org

your number and we can talk on the phone sometime." I saw nothing wrong with that. She was cool enough and cute.

Then next thing I knew she started to fall asleep next to me. I tried to wake her up, and she pulled me towards her. We stared in each other's eyes for a hot second, and before I knew it she was kissing my cheek. So me being drunk, and she being drunk, we did our thang.

I felt weird after we had sex. I hadn't had a one-night stand before. I felt I straight up took advantage of her, and that seemed strange. After we were done, I left her and we never spoke again. But we kept hearing about each other through mutual friends. I just thought of her as a female I met at a party.

> I knew if I became a father, my teenage life was gone.

My Girl Helped Me Think

But now she had called me, nine months later, telling me a baby had come out of that night and that it would be in the world in a week. I felt very confused and I wanted to punch something.

Instead, I called my girl, who I had only recently started seeing, and told her what was going down. My lady sounded stunned on the phone but helped me think through the situation.

We both thought that the first thing I needed to do was to take a paternity test to see if the kid was really mine. We weren't ready yet to think too far beyond that. I kept asking myself, "What if it is mine? Am I ready to be a father? Am I ready to take care of another life? How would I ever handle getting along with the kid's mother, someone who would be there in the kid's life forever, someone I couldn't stand for putting me through this?"

I Wouldn't Abandon My Child

I did know that if it was mine, I wasn't going to abandon it. I've seen too many fathers leave their kids behind. In fact, my own father left me behind when he went to jail.

I knew the pain of growing up without a dad, and I always swore I wouldn't do that if I had a child. So I knew if I became a father, my teenage life was gone. I would have to stop acting like a boy and take care of my responsibilities as a man.

I didn't know what that meant, exactly. I didn't know whether it meant I would have to quit school to get a full-time job. I did know I was too young for this. What's worse, I didn't have a penny to my name. But the baby would need things: diapers, a crib, toys, clothes, milk.

I Felt Ashamed

So many thoughts in my head, so many things to do, and the way I saw it was I didn't have much time to do those things. The walls were closing quick and I felt I had no one to help me.

I couldn't go back to selling products on the street. What good would I be to my kid if I were dead or locked up? I couldn't go to my parents— they would kill me. How the hell could I tell my moms that I had a kid? How could I tell any of my family members?

I felt ashamed. I was supposed to be the one who succeeded, who didn't get caught in situations like this.

Mad at Her, Mad at Myself

Melanie called me back and asked why I hung up on her. I told her, "You knew all this and held out on me for this long, and you wondering why I am being mean to you? I want nothing to do with you. I want to be with my lady and that's it. The only reason I am going be nice to you and show some respect towards you is for the kid."

I knew I was half responsible for all this and that made me even more mad. I wanted to hit someone, anyone. I wanted to slap her through the damn phone, but I don't hit females.

At the time it was around graduation, and I had to pass the tests I needed to graduate. As I was studying for the tests and, later, taking them, my mind was on the baby. I could think of nothing but the baby, my girl, my family and how was I gonna make money.

For a while I thought that my girl would leave, too, for the simple fact that females hate dealing with baby mama drama. Still, she continued to stand by me.

My friends who I told about the baby situation were shocked about the news, but they supported me 100%. I couldn't ask for better friends in a time of need.

I Knew Parenting Was Hard

But that didn't mean everything was good. I was nervous just thinking about becoming a father, and even with the best friends and girl in the world, I wasn't ready.

I had an idea how hard it is to be a good parent. After all, neither of my parents pulled it off well enough to keep me at home, and so I ended up in foster care. It hurt that my father had always been in and out of my life.

> **I sat there holding Shorty in my arms like a prized possession. The last time I saw a baby that beautiful was when my lil' sister was born.**

So when I'd thought of having kids myself, I wanted everything to be perfect. I wanted to have two seeds, a boy and a girl, or as I would call them, my prince and princess. I pictured having my seeds by the wife I chose to marry and that I would be financially stable enough to take care of them. Not to have everything completely opposite—to have a kid by someone who I don't care for, and to raise a kid when I'm not stable.

I Held Shorty in My Arms

On Thursday, June 20, Melanie had the baby. She called me two hours after she delivered and told me that it was a boy. I was happy to hear that it had gone well with her and that the baby was healthy.

I went to the hospital that Friday to take the paternity test. As he took some blood for my DNA, the doctor said the results wouldn't be ready for a few days. I felt weird having the blood drawn; my arm was flinching as he did it. I couldn't stop thinking about how all of this was happening so fast.

Afterward I went to see the baby. He was sleeping and beautiful. The last time I saw a baby that beautiful was when my lil' sister was born. I asked the nurse could I hold him, and she gave me the baby.

I sat there holding Shorty in my arms like a prized possession. I started talking to the baby like I already knew it was mine. He was cute, with hazel eyes, a little hair and little hands and feet.

I Wouldn't Let Him Down

When the nurse told me that she had to put him back in the crib, I didn't want to let him go. The whole feeling that the baby was mine hit me hard. I saw Shorty's eyes and I knew that he was my responsibility and I wouldn't let him down.

The whole time I was in the hospital room, Melanie and I didn't communicate. The only time we spoke was when it regarded the baby. I told Melanie, "My only plans are to raise that baby, nothing else." She said she understood that.

I told her I would get the diapers and some toys, though I still hadn't figured out how. She said she and her mother would supply the clothes and the crib and I could see the kid whenever I wanted.

I said I'd see Shorty after school and some nights that I had free. Melanie's moms was in the hospital, too. She seemed to like me, but she was also mad at me because she knew that we were too young and that we weren't ready for this.

Monday was the big day, the day I'd find out if the kid was really mine. At the end of the day, I was supposed to meet my lady and tell her the results.

When I got to the hospital, I saw Shorty moving, and I asked the doctor if I could hold him while he went and got the results. So I sat there in a chair holding Shorty in my arms, rocking back and forth.

The Kid Is Not My Son?

I started talking to him, telling him, "Hey, little one, I might be your father," and, "Don't worry, I will never leave you." I knew I was getting a little too mushy with Shorty, but I couldn't help it. I even felt the urge to cry and let some feelings out.

The way the baby moved in my arms was a joyous feeling to me. He was lying there sleeping, eyes closed, his little fists tight. I couldn't believe this was mine.

After a while, Melanie caught my attention. She was just outside the room, and I saw that she was crying. Her mother got up and started yelling at the doctor, "It has to be him." I walked toward them, and as the yelling got louder, the baby started crying and the nurse took him away.

Melanie's mother told the doctor, "I'll pay you to tell him he is the father." I couldn't believe what I was hearing. Then I felt like I was about to flip out on her.

As I struggled to stay calm, the doctor pulled me to the side and told me eye to eye, face to face, that the child wasn't mine. I felt strange—both sad and overjoyed. I knew I wasn't ready to be a father, but I had been liking the idea of having a kid to call mine.

That night, I told my girl the news. She was glad. But later as I walked down the streets, I noticed all the babies who were with their fathers, and I started to miss Shorty. It was strange, all I'd been through in the last week because of that one-night mistake with Melanie. It was stranger to think that I could've been a father.

I'm More Cautious About Sex

I call Melanie up once in a while to check up on Shorty. See how he's holding up. I was mad at her for doing all that to me, but I came out all right and she is having to give up her teen years.

I believe some good has come out of it for me. My lady and I are stronger as a couple after going through that together, and I'm much more cautious about sex. Let's just say I always use a condom. I know that having kids isn't my thing, not now. (Maybe when I am about 22 and financially stable, I'll think about it.)

After seeing Shorty and holding him in my arms, I see the love fathers have for their kids. But I also see why so many run. It's frightening to look at something so small and know how much it needs you. But that don't make it right for fathers to leave.

All About Birth Control, Right Here

By RASHEEDA RAJI and KYMBERLY SHECKLEFORD

You must have heard it time and time again, but we're going to let you know one more time: abstinence, not having sexual intercourse, is the only 100% sure method of avoiding getting pregnant or contracting sexually transmitted diseases (STDs), including HIV, the virus that causes AIDS. But if you do decide to have sex, protect yourself and your body by knowing how to get and use condoms.

Each year, nearly four million STD infections are caught by teenagers in the United States. Sexually active teenage girls in the U.S. who don't practice safe sex, which means sex with a condom, have a 90% chance of becoming pregnant within a year of first having intercourse.

By using birth control and condoms together, you reduce two risks at once: the chance that you'll get an STD and the chance you'll have an unwanted pregnancy.

On the next few pages, we've provided information about both the male and female condom and the pill. We've also explained how various female contraceptives work, such as the patch, the diaphragm and the sponge. We're hoping that these facts will help you make informed decisions about your sex life.

But the tough news is that even the combination of birth control and condoms won't give you 100% protection against pregnancy. The only surefire way to get that is to avoid genital-to-genital contact.

Because you are putting your body on the line for someone else, consider talking to your partner about birth control and condoms before you start messing around. Get familiar with one another's sexual history. Share your feelings and concerns about sexual activity. You want to make sure that you are making a decision that you won't regret later.

If you become sexually active, you're exposing yourself to a whole new range of possible medical conditions. It's more important than ever to maintain your health. If you're a woman, get regular gynecological

www.youthcomm.org

(GYN) examinations and STD tests. If you're a man, get tested regularly for STDs.

Planned Parenthood offers confidential services to teens regardless of age or income, including GYN exams, all kinds of contraceptives, family planning counseling, emergency birth control, pregnancy testing, prenatal care, abortions, and STD and HIV testing. For the Planned Parenthood nearest to you, call 1-800-230-PLAN or check www.plannedparenthood. org

The Condom

Description: A cover, usually made of latex, that fits over the penis and catches semen before, during and after a man ejaculates, preventing sperm from entering his partner's body. (Some condoms are made of animal tissue, like "lambskin," but these don't help prevent the spread of HIV and AIDS.)

The condom is the only male contraceptive currently available. The condom (for men) and the female condom are the only contraceptives that protect against STDs.

Effectiveness: Of 100 women whose partners use condoms when they have sex, about 15 will become pregnant during the first year of typical use. Typical use rates take into account that most people won't use condoms

correctly every time. Only two will become pregnant if condoms are used perfectly.

Because condoms help protect against HIV and other infections as well as against pregnancy, anyone who is sexually active or thinking of having vaginal or anal sex should use (or ask their partners) to use them.

Because it can break or slip off if not used correctly, the condom is more effective as birth control when used with a spermicidal (sperm-killing) foam, film, cream, insert or jelly.

Pros: Condoms help prevent the spread of HIV and other STDs. They are inexpensive and easy to get. You can buy them at any drugstore without a prescription, and many clinics and some high schools make them available for free.

Since condoms are small and lightweight, it's easy to carry them with you at all times. They make it possible for men to take responsibility for birth control. They may also help a man stay erect longer.

Cons: You have to use one every time you have intercourse. Putting the condom on may feel awkward or uncomfortable at first since it must be used right at the time of intercourse. It may also dull sensation for either partner. It may burst or come off during intercourse, especially if it's not put on correctly (see directions below).

Possible Side Effects: There are none, except for people who are allergic to latex. (They can use plastic condoms, which are just as effective as latex.)

Cost: The price per dozen ranges from $7-$12, depending on the brand, but you can often get them free at clinics.

Spermicide

Description: Spermicide is the term used for any sperm-killing chemical— nonoxynol-9 is the most common. It comes in many forms, including film, inserts (also called suppositories), foam, cream and jelly.

Spermicide should be used with another form of contraception such as condoms. If you're using a condom, apply spermicide as well, to increase protection against pregnancy.

Effectiveness: With typical use, 29 of 100 women will get pregnant. With perfect use, 15 will become pregnant. Condoms increase effectiveness.

Pros: Application is quick and simple. You can use spermicide 15-30 minutes before you have sex and be ready to go.

Cons: Spermicide provides no protection against HIV or other STDs. It's only effective for an hour after insertion. If not used properly, spermicidal cream and jelly can be messy.

Possible Side Effects: The most common side effects are burning and itching. If any other symptoms occur, stop using it immediately and call a doctor.

Price: An applicator kit of foam or jelly costs about $8. Refills cost $4-$8. A single application of film or an insert costs about $1, and they're usually sold in packs of three or more.

The Female Condom

Description: A plastic baggie-like pouch that has flexible rings on each end. The female condom is made of latex. One ring is inserted deep into the vagina and the other ring stays open outside the vagina. The rings help to hold the condom in place.

The female condom collects semen before, during and after ejaculation, keeping sperm from entering the vagina and protecting against pregnancy.

Female condoms should not be used at the same time as male condoms.

Effectiveness: Female condoms are typically 79% effective in preventing pregnancy. With perfect use, they can be 95% effective.

Pros: Because the female condom helps prevent many sexually transmitted infections (including HIV and AIDS), any heterosexual female should consider using it. Anyone—man or woman—who is going to have anal sex should also consider it.

The female condom can be purchased at a drugstore without a prescription.

Cons: Female condoms can sometimes be tricky to use.

Female condoms can be about three times more expensive than male condoms. In addition, unlike many male condoms, many female condoms don't come with spermicide.

Possible Side Effects: Condoms have no side effects except for people who are allergic to latex. They may use plastic condoms instead.

Price: Female condoms start at about $3 each. Some family planning centers give them away or charge very little.

The Pill

Description: A monthly series of pills—you take one birth control tablet a day. Basically, the Pill tricks your body into thinking it's already pregnant so you can't get pregnant.

Effectiveness: Eight of every 100 women who use the Pill will get pregnant during the first year of typical use. Women who use it correctly, taking it every day, have less than a 1% chance of getting pregnant.

However, it may take a week or two for the Pill to become effective.

Pros: The Pill is good for women who are disciplined (because you have to remember to take it at the same time every day—missing a pill can lead to pregnancy).

Women who use the Pill have more regular periods, less menstrual flow, less cramping, less iron deficiency and anemia, less pelvic inflammatory disease (PID) and less premenstrual tension than women who don't take it.

Cons: The Pill doesn't protect against HIV or other STDs.

You need a doctor's prescription to get the Pill.

You must take it every day at the same time, even when you aren't planning to have sex.

Women who take it may be at slightly greater risk for some diseases—ask your doctor about this.

Possible Side Effects: Many women don't have any side effects, and for those who do, most side effects go away after two or three months. The Pill can cause nausea, vomiting, headaches, weight gain or loss, breast tenderness or bleeding between periods.

Price: The Pill can be purchased at a drugstore or clinic for $25-$40 per month. You must have a prescription.

The Patch

Description: The patch is a thin piece of plastic no bigger than a matchbook. Like the Pill and the ring, the patch stops your ovaries from producing eggs. The patch is worn on the buttocks, stomach, upper arm or upper torso (but never on the breasts).

Use one patch per week for three weeks in a row. On the fourth week, do NOT wear a patch. Your menstrual period should start. Apply a new patch seven days later to start another month of birth control.

For the first seven days of a new patch cycle, you may not be protected from pregnancy. Use backup methods of birth control for seven days.

Effectiveness: You must have the patch firmly attached to your skin—it won't work if it's loose or falls off for longer than 24 hours.

With typical use, eight women out of 100 will get pregnant while using the patch. With perfect use, fewer than one out of 100 women will become pregnant.

Pros: The patch is convenient and easy to use. It makes your period more regular, lighter and shorter. Like the ring, the patch stops your fertility for only one month at a time.

Cons: The patch does not protect you from HIV and STDs.

You must see a doctor to get the patch. Like the ring, if you weigh more than 198 lbs or if you've had certain medical conditions, you shouldn't use the patch.

Possible Side Effects: As with the ring, women who experience any of the following symptoms while wearing the patch should call a doctor immediately: severe abdominal (stomach) pains, chest pain or shortness of breath, severe headaches, eye problems (like blurred vision), severe leg or arm pain, or numbness in the arms or legs.

Side effects, which should clear up after two or three months, may include bleeding between periods, weight gain or loss, breast tenderness, nausea and mood swings.

Price: The patches are $30-$35 a month.

The Sponge

Description: It's a soft polyurethane foam sponge containing spermicide, shaped a bit like a two-inch wide single earmuff. It prevents sperm from entering the cervix and reaching the egg.

Before intercourse, you moisten the sponge with water and then insert it deep into your vagina, where it fits snugly against your cervix. It has a nylon loop attached to the bottom so you can remove it. The sponge must be left in for at least six hours after intercourse, and removed within 30 hours.

Effectiveness: With typical use, 13-16 out of 100 women will get pregnant. With perfect use, 9-11 women will get pregnant.

Pros: You don't need a prescription or a fitting to use the sponge.

You can insert it hours before intercourse, and it can be used for 24 hours through repeated acts of intercourse. There are no messy gels or foams you have to add to it. Generally, neither you nor your partner will feel it.

Since it's small, you can carry it around discreetly. It has no effect on your natural hormones.

Cons: The sponge doesn't protect against STDs. Some women have trouble inserting or removing the sponge.

You should NOT use the sponge during any of the following conditions: while you have your period, if you have a urinary tract infection, if you're allergic to polyurethane, spermicide or sulfa drugs, or if you've recently had an abortion, childbirth or miscarriage.

Possible Side Effects: Some people experience vaginal irritation while using the sponge.

Sponge users may be at a slightly higher risk of toxic shock syndrome, a serious illness caused by bacteria (also associated with the use of highly absorbent tampons). Be sure to remove the sponge within 30 hours to minimize this risk.

Price: It costs about $7.50-$10 for a package of three at drugstores.

www.youthcomm.org

The Cervical Cap

Description: A small silicone cup that you insert deep in the vagina to fit right over your cervix, creating an almost airtight seal. It should be used with a spermicidal cream or jelly.

Effectiveness: With typical use, 14 out of 100 women who use the cap will become pregnant, provided they've never been pregnant or given birth. For women who have given birth vaginally, 29 out of 100 will become pregnant.

Pros: The cervical cap may be left in place for up to 48 hours. You can insert it up to 40 hours before intercourse, and you should leave it in for at least six to eight hours afterward.

Like the diaphragm, the cervical cap is good for someone who's comfortable with her body and feels confident about being able to use it every time she has sex.

The cervical cap requires less spermicide than a diaphragm so it's less messy and less expensive to use.

Because it's smaller than the diaphragm, it may be more comfortable. And since you can put it in way ahead of time, many women find it more convenient to use.

The cervical cap has no long-term impact on fertility; if you want to get pregnant, stop using it.

Cons: It does not provide protection against HIV and other STDs.

You must see a doctor to get a cervical cap. Not all women can get one that fits properly. Some women find it difficult to put in. It's not good for someone who's uncomfortable or embarrassed about touching herself.

It's not as widely available as the diaphragm.

It must be used every time you have intercourse. It may become dislodged during intercourse.

Possible Side Effects: An unpleasant odor can result when the cervical cap is worn for more than 48 hours.

Price: About $30-$50 for the cervical cap, and the cost of spermicide.

Depo-provera

Description: Depo-Provera is a shot that you get injected into your system every 12 weeks with a needle. Depo-Provera keeps the ovaries from releasing eggs.

Effectiveness: Out of every 1,000 women who use Depo-Provera correctly and consistently for a year, only three will get pregnant. Three out of every 100 women will become pregnant with typical use.

Pros: Depo-Provera is convenient in that it prevents pregnancy for 12 weeks at a time; it does not need to be taken daily or used at the time of intercourse. It begins working almost immediately if you take the shot during the first five days of your period. Otherwise, it takes a week to become effective. To be safe you should wait 24 hours after an injection before having sex.

Depo-Provera can reduce menstrual cramps and anemia and protect against ovarian cysts.

Cons: Depo-Provera doesn't protect against HIV or other STDs.

Depo-Provera must be administered by a doctor every three months.

If you don't like it and want to stop using it, you'll have to suffer from any side effects you've been experiencing for up to three months while waiting for your last injection to wear off.

You should not use it continuously for more than two years.

Possible Side Effects: Irregular periods are common.

Less common side effects may include increased appetite and weight gain, headache, sore breasts, nausea, nervousness, dizziness, depression, skin rashes or spotty darkening of the skin, hair loss, increased hair on face or body, and increased or decreased sex drive.

Price: The initial visit is $35-$125 and injections are $30-$15.

The Ring

Description: A soft and flexible plastic ring that's inserted into the vagina. Like the patch and the Pill, the ring (also called the vaginal ring) releases synthetic hormones to prevent pregnancy.

Effectiveness: The ring is similar to the patch in this area.

Pros: Only one ring is needed for three weeks of use, though you must remember to remove it exactly 21 days after you put it in, and replace it one week after that. Inserting the ring may be awkward at first. However, since the ring is not a barrier method like the diaphragm, incorrect placement is not usually a problem.

Cons: The ring doesn't protect you from STDs. You need to store the ring at room temperature (no more than 77° F) and away from direct sunlight. It's possible for the ring to slip out of the vagina. If this happens, you can wash the ring with cold to lukewarm (not hot) water and put it back in.

If more than three hours pass without the ring in your vagina, there is a chance you'll become pregnant if you have sex. The ring must be worn continuously for seven days to regain effectiveness.

As with the patch, if you weigh more than 198 lbs or if you've had any of the following medical conditions, you shouldn't use it: uncontrolled high blood pressure, clots or vein inflammation, heart attack or stroke, vaginal bleeding, an abnormal growth or cancer of the breast or uterus, liver disease, diabetes, or migraine headaches with aura.

Possible Side Effects: Women who experience any of the following symptoms while wearing a vaginal ring should call a doctor immediately: severe abdominal (stomach) pains, chest pain or shortness of breath, severe headaches, eye problems (like blurred vision), severe leg or arm pain, or numbness in the arms or legs.

Side effects may include mood swings, headache, nausea, vaginal discharge, breast tenderness, weight gain or loss, bleeding between periods, and vaginal irritation.

Price: The ring costs $30-$35 a month.

The Diaphragm

Description: A soft silicone or latex cup that you fill with spermicidal cream or jelly. It's inserted into the vagina to cover the opening of the uterus (which is called the cervix). The diaphragm forms a barrier that prevents sperm from entering the uterus and fertilizing an egg.

Effectiveness: Out of 100 women who use them, 16 will become pregnant during the first year of typical use. With perfect use, six out of 100 will become pregnant.

Pros: There are almost no side effects or health risks. You can insert it up to six hours before intercourse, so you don't have to worry that putting it in will "ruin the moment."

The diaphragm is good for someone who's comfortable with her body, and who feels confident about being able to use it every time she has sex.

Cons: The diaphragm doesn't protect against HIV and other STDs.

You must see a doctor to get one. not good for someone who's uncomfortable or embarrassed about touching herself or who would find it a hassle to deal with every time she has sex.

You have to use it every time you have sex. You must put it in no more than six hours before having sex and you must leave it in for at least six hours afterward. If you have intercourse more than once while the diaphragm is in, you need to insert more spermicide each time.

You need to wash, rinse and dry it carefully after each use and store it away from light.

It must be checked from time to time for weak spots or tiny holes. The size should be checked every year (your size may change after gaining or losing a lot of weight, giving birth or having an abortion).

The spermicide can be messy, and you may be drippy after use.

Possible Side Effects: If left in your body for more than 24 hours, the diaphragm can cause bacterial infections or increase your risk of toxic shock syndrome. It can be difficult to remove if it's not put in properly.

Price: The diaphragm itself costs $15 or more and is good for an average of two years. But you must also add the cost of spermicidal jelly or cream (from about $8 to $18 a tube, depending on the size, and the tube lasts a while).

Not Too Late: The Morning After Pill

If a condom breaks or you have unprotected sex, it's still possible to protect yourself from getting pregnant (but not from getting an STD) by taking the "morning after pill," also known as emergency contraception.

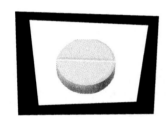

You can use emergency contraception up to five days after having unprotected sex. However, the sooner you take these pills, the more likely they'll prevent pregnancy.

Emergency contraception pills work in a few ways. They can stop an egg and sperm from meeting, or stop the egg from attaching to the uterus so you can't get pregnant.

Emergency contraception shouldn't be used instead of birth-control because it's not healthy to take it often and it's not as effective as many other kinds of birth control—it prevents pregnancy only 75–89% of the time.

Emergency contraception pills are available by prescription. However, you can get a prescription pretty quickly by making an appointment at Planned Parenthood. Call 1-888-NOT-2-LATE.

Back in the Stirrups— Again

Taking the pelvic exam, step-by-step.

By MADELEINE GORDILLO

Your visit to the gynecologist begins like any doctor's appointment—you fill out forms about your medical history and your reasons for being there. There are many clinics where you can get exams for free, but you may be required to show identification. (Call 1-800-230-PLAN to find a clinic near you.)

At the clinic, you may be asked for blood or urine samples to test for pregnancy and infection. At some clinics, you speak to a counselor before getting examined by a doctor or nurse-practitioner. The counselor, or sometimes the practitioner, reads your form and may ask for more information. (For example, if there is diabetes in your family, she'll ask which family member has it.) She will also ask why you are there and if you have any questions. If you came for something specific, like birth control, or to find out if you have a sexually transmitted infection, you should tell her that.

The Stirrups

After the counseling session, you go into an exam room, where you are asked to take off your clothes and change into a paper robe. The exam table has metal hoops, called stirrups, attached to the bottom corners.

The examination begins with a breast exam. The doctor will open your robe and tell you to place both hands behind your head. Using the flat side of her three middle fingers, she'll feel for any abnormal lumps in your breasts and armpits. The doctor should also teach you how to examine your own breasts between doctors' visits.

The Speculum

Next comes the pelvic exam. This is when the practitioner asks you to lay down and put your heels in the stirrups. They keep your legs spread apart enough so that the doctor will be able to examine you properly.

The doctor will check the outer surface of your vagina to make sure everything looks healthy. Then she inserts the speculum, an instrument used to hold the walls of the vagina open so the doctor can see inside. The doctor will gently insert the speculum into your vagina. Once it's in place, she will open the mouth of the speculum. Many people fear that this will be painful, but if you relax and don't tense up, all you should feel is a slight pressure.

The doctor will check the walls of your vagina and the opening of your cervix for any abnormalities (redness, inflammation, cysts, unusual discharge) that could be signs of infection or disease. If you have any questions about your reproductive organs or about what the doctor is doing, you should feel free to ask them during the exam.

The Pap Smear

Next, the doctor will insert a long Q-tip into your vagina to get some cell samples. (You might feel some "poking" at this point.) This is called the Pap smear and it is done to test for warning signs of cancer. If you are sexually active, she will take another sample to test you for gonorrhea and chlamydia. This lasts about a minute. Then the doctor closes the speculum and eases it out.

Next she changes her gloves and spreads lubricant on one or two of her fingers and puts them inside your vagina to feel your cervix and internal organs. You will feel a little pressure at this point. With her other hand, the doctor will press down on your lower abdomen to feel your uterus and ovaries. She does this to feel for any abnormal swelling, tenderness or lumps.

The Results

The doctor will probably spend a few minutes discussing your exam with you when she's done. You will be told if anything abnormal was found during the exam, such as inflammation of the vagina, any unusual lumps or discharge. The doctor might prescribe something for you or tell you that you need additional tests. Don't expect the results of your Pap smear and STD culture right away. That usually takes a few days. If anything irregular shows up in those test results, she'll contact you. If you don't hear from her, and you weren't told to call for the results, then everything's fine.

To stay healthy, doctors recommend that everyone have a physical exam every year.

To find out more about teen sexual health, check out www.teenwire.com. To learn about confidentiality laws where you live log on to www.sxetc.org and click on your state.

Date with Destiny

My boyfriend told me he didn't have HIV. He lied.

By XAVIER REYES

Let me tell you about the day that changed my destiny. It was July 30, 1998. Ten days after I turned 20 years old. I was working for the Gay Men's Health Crisis and living in an apartment that was a part of the Supervised Independent Living Program. I was excited about moving out on my own within a year. Little did I know how my life was going to change on this day.

Xavier Reyes

Let's backtrack a little. Two weeks before, I had gotten tested for HIV. I began to get tested when I was 16 years old because I was engaging in sex and sometimes I didn't use a condom. I wanted to be sure that I hadn't gotten infected.

It wasn't a big deal because I had gotten tested many times before and always got a negative result, meaning I didn't have HIV. And since the last time I'd been tested, the only person I'd had sex without a condom with was someone I'd been in a long-term relationship with. He assured me that he had been tested for HIV and that he did not have it. And even though he refused to show me the test results, I trusted him, so I believed him. He had been asking me to have unprotected sex for some time, and I eventually gave in to his request. The condoms went out the window for the duration of our relationship.

I Took the Test for HIV...Again

After about a year and a half, our relationship ended. He had become way too controlling for me. He didn't want me to go out with my friends or do the things I used to do before I met him. The last straw for me was when he told me that he needed to "mold" me into the person he wanted me to be. I told him to get some clay and mold his next boyfriend. I walked out and that was that. It wasn't long before I was over him and loving being single.

So back to July 30. It was a hot summer day. I went to work as usual. Nothing was different except for me having to get back my HIV results. I had taken the test in the HIV testing center of the agency where I worked. When it was time to go see what my results were, I said a prayer and ran down the two flights of stairs to the sixth floor.

Waiting for the Results

The receptionist told me to have a seat and someone would be with me. I sat and began to thumb through a magazine. I didn't read any of the articles, because though I wasn't really worried, I always felt a little anxiety wondering what the results of my HIV test would be. I began to recall the times that I had not practiced safe sex in my life. Then I reminded myself that I had only done that with people who I knew were HIV negative. After all, I had asked them.

"Excuse me, Xavier?" a voice called out, interrupting my thoughts.

It was the director of the department. It was agency policy for employees to the see the director for test results. She was a very pleasant woman who could have you feeling like her best friend within the first few minutes of meeting her.

> **I needed to breathe. I was in shock. How? Why? But most of all, who? Who gave me HIV?**

I'd Heard It All Before

I stood and shook her hand. "Let's go into my office so we can have a little more privacy," she said. I followed her into the office and we made small talk. She opened a drawer and took out a file.

She began to go over the routine stuff, telling me what the three possible test results were, the stuff you hear every time you get tested for HIV. It was either: an HIV negative result, meaning I didn't have HIV; an HIV inconclusive result, meaning the test was unable tell whether I had HIV, and I would need to be tested again; or an HIV positive result, meaning I had somehow contracted HIV.

As she went on, I got more and more anxious. I really just wanted to know what the results were. After all, I'd heard this stuff a million times before.

Soon she was telling me what I would need to do if I was negative. "Be sure to continue practicing safe sex, get tested in six months, and be with only one partner," she said, sounding like a mother telling me to wear clean socks.

'Your Results Came Back...'

Then she started talking about what I would need to do if I tested positive for HIV. I tuned her out because I didn't want to think about what it would be like and how my life would change if I did have HIV.

"OK, and now for your results," she said.

"Ladies and gentlemen, the envelope please," I thought to myself.

She opened the file and placed it on her desk. As always, I was officially nervous. No matter how many times I'd done this before, I couldn't help but feel anxious those last few minutes right before I found out if my life was going to change or stay the same.

Who Gave Me HIV?

"Xavier, your results came back positive," she blurted.

The blood ran from my body. A wave of nerves washed over me. I needed to breathe. I was in shock. How? Why? But most of all, who? Who gave me HIV?

I swallowed and tried to compose myself. I kept telling myself to breathe. Why me? I was so young. After breaking up with my boyfriend, I was looking forward to a new life, a second chance at living again. I was wrecked. I felt as if I had let down people who cared about me. I felt guilty for being gay. I felt like this was a punishment from God. I did everything possible to prevent myself from crying.

Not Now

"Are you OK?" she was asking.

"Yeah, fine." It was a lie, of course.

"I think it may be a good idea if you take the rest of the day off. If you have the time, you might want to take a few days off to relax and absorb this. This is not going to be easy for you, but you can do it. Understand that this does not mean a death sentence."

She started explaining that the results were not going to be shown to anyone without my permission. Everything else she said was just a blur. I couldn't listen anymore. I needed to leave. I wanted to go home and crawl up in bed. I didn't want to think about this. Not now.

I went straight to my boss's office. I told her what had happened and that I needed to leave immediately. She was understanding, and allowed me to take off the next two days. I went outside and walked around aimlessly for two hours.

Shock, Anger and Betrayal

I was angry, so angry. I didn't know what to do with myself so I tried calling my ex to tell him what had happened. I was confident that he was the one who infected me. He was the only one who I had been with for over a year and a half.

> **'How could you do this? I asked you over and over if you were HIV negative and you lied to me!'**

I finally reached him and told him about the test. To add insult to injury, he was more concerned about who I had told than how I was doing. He didn't want any of my friends getting revenge on him.

I told him I was on my way over. By the time I got to his house, I was fuming mad. I wanted answers and I wanted them yesterday.

"How could you do this to me?" I asked.

"Who did you tell?" he still wanted to know.

"What does it matter? I told those who are concerned about me."

"You shouldn't have done that. Why didn't you call me first? We could have handled this together."

'You Lied to Me'

"No, we couldn't have," I replied, getting more agitated by the moment. "Look, all I want to know is, are you positive?"

"Uh, yeah, I just got tested recently and I found out I was positive."

"You what?" My voice was getting louder and I was beginning to get choked up. I couldn't believe this was happening. "I think you are lying and I also think that you've been positive longer than you say you have. How could you do this? I asked you over and over if you were negative and you lied to me! What am I supposed to do now?"

Emotions Swirling in My Head

"Listen, baby, we can work this out." He tried to pull me closer to him.

"Get off of me! There is nothing to work out!" I pulled away from him. I had heard enough. I wanted to get out. "F-ck you! Don't ever bother me again!" I screamed. I was crying now. There was nothing more to say or do. I picked up my book bag, wiped my face with my shirt and stormed out of his house. My head was pounding. I could hear him calling me to come back. I kept walking.

I went home and got in bed. I couldn't eat. I felt as if my life had stopped. I had so many emotions swirling in my head that I could not even think straight.

As I lay in my bed, I remembered all the people I already knew who were living with HIV. They were able to do everything they wanted to do in their lives. Nothing stopped them. Their sense of humor about it also helped them to deal with it better. Remembering them made me feel a little calmer.

I knew I could talk to them about what I was going through. I also knew I had many other people who could help support me. I kept telling myself that I was fortunate to have tested positive in 1998 and not 1988, a time when little was known about HIV and there were very few medications available.

Hoping It's a Bad Dream

But I was also pissed off. Although the responsibility of deciding to have unsafe sex fell in my lap, I was angry because I had given my ex the benefit of the doubt. I had trusted him. And he had failed me. I felt like he took my life away from me.

I wanted to get even with him for lying to me. But deep inside, I knew that revenge would get me nowhere. Even after I did get my revenge, I would still be HIV positive. Nothing could change that. Not now.

I fell asleep hoping that when I awoke, this day would have been a dream.

Learning to Deal

After several weeks, once the initial shock of learning that I was positive wore off, I began looking for ways that I could improve my life, both physically and emotionally. I'd never allowed any challenge in my life to take me down before and I was not about to let this one be the first.

I began to go to therapy to help myself deal with being HIV positive. Therapy taught me that although I may be faced with a life-threatening illness, I shouldn't use it as a reason for not trying to achieve the things I want in life. In fact, it should be the reason for achieving the goals I want, such as finishing college and moving out of New York. Therapy also helped me accept that being positive was not a punishment from God for being gay. My therapist told me, "God doesn't give nothing you can't handle." It was then that I promised myself that I would not give up without a fight.

I started spending a lot of time alone, just looking at my life. If I wanted to live longer, I knew that I needed to spend more time on me and less time in the clubs. I needed to make sure that I got enough rest, reduced my stress and took my medications.

Above all, though, I needed to practice safe sex at all times. I did not want to infect another person. I did not want to live the rest of my days knowing that I was responsible for that.

Working Towards My Dreams

I went back to college soon after finding out that I was HIV positive. I wrote a final report, which was close to 175 pages, about learning to cope with HIV. Part of the final report required me to do journal entries to help me deal with the feelings I was having around being positive. Writing the paper and those journal entries really helped me put what happened to me over the past year into perspective. It helped me realize how strong a person I really was. It also helped me find ways of coping, such as exercising, talking more with my friends, and taking acupuncture when life was getting too stressful for me.

I got an A+ on the paper and was the only student in my class to make it onto the dean's list that semester.

This past summer marked three years since I learned that I was positive. I am now working as the administrative director for a community foundation, and am still trying to finish that college degree. My viral load is undetectable, which means that the amount of HIV in my body is so low that the current available tests cannot detect it. It does not mean that I am negative, it just means that there isn't a lot of HIV in my system. This is due, in part, to me taking my medications and living a healthier life.

Forgiving Myself For Being HIV Positive

More important, I have gradually managed to come to terms with my HIV status. I've learned to forgive myself for being HIV positive. I don't consider this a punishment from God. I consider it sort of like a tap on the shoulder telling me that I need to take better care of myself and not be so reckless with my life because I only have one shot at living.

Believe it or not, I also forgave the person who infected me. I had the opportunity to protect myself and I chose not to. I can live with that. Being angry at him or trying to be vengeful towards him will not make the HIV leave my body. I want to live a happy life, not a bitter one. Although he is no longer in my life, I know that I would be able to see him in the street and not want to get into a fistfight with him.

One of the major concerns I had when I became infected was whether I would be able to find a new boyfriend who would love and accept me even though I had HIV. Thankfully, I have been blessed with a boyfriend who does. When he and I first met, I was scared to tell him because I did not want to be rejected. But I wanted to tell him because I did not want to mislead him. When I did tell him, I was surprised by his reaction. Not only did he say that he was cool with it, but he also told me that he was very happy that I'd told him. We have now been together a year and three months and we are living together. Yes, you can say happily ever after.

Grateful for What I Have

I have learned to be grateful for what I have now that I'm living with HIV. The expensive medications I need are covered by my health insurance. There are so many in this world who don't even know they have HIV, or don't have access to the costly care they need. Even though

I have an illness that is fatal, I am better off than a lot people. I can see, walk and talk. I am able to work and provide for myself. By taking a step back and counting my blessings, I have been able to see that I am not that bad off.

I am looking forward to living a healthy, long life. My doctor tells me that if I take my medications and follow his orders, he can help me live to the age of 60. I am confident that this will happen. And with all the research going on about HIV, maybe, just maybe, they might come up with a cure.

Activity Page for Group Leaders

Learning About Safe Sex and Abstinence

Topic: Safe sex and abstinence

Goal: Reinforce need for condom use. Reinforce idea that only no sex is truly safe sex. Reinforce how STDs are spread from person to person to person.

What You'll Need: pens/pencils

Enough index cards for the group

Mark three of the cards as follows:

■ Place an "X" in the corner of one card. (This is the "HIV positive person.")

■ Write a C in the corner of one card (for condom use or safer sex practitioner.)

■ On one card write "DO NOT WRITE YOUR NAME ON ANY CARD AND DO NOT LET ANYONE WRITE THEIR NAME ON YOUR CARD." (This is the "abstinent person")

■ Write "B" on the rest of the cards for birth control other than condom use.

■ Keep the "X" card for yourself.

Time: 45 minutes

Activity: 30 minutes

■ **Give each student a card.** Tell them they have three minutes to walk around and get three other students and you, the teacher, to sign their cards. After they are done they should go back to their seat. (Do not tell them at this time what the letters mean.)

■ **Tell the students that the X on your card means you are HIV positive.** Remind them what this means. (If any student reacts strongly to your announcement—makes a sound of disgust or a nervous giggle—ask that student why they responded that way. This can be a good opportunity to have a short discussion about students' fears and attitudes.)

■ **Read the names on your card and ask them to please stand.** Everyone still seated should read the names on their cards. If any of them have the names of people who are standing then they must stand. Continue with the process until all students are standing except the "abstinent person."

■ **Tell the students** that for the purpose of this exercise, writing their names on cards or having other people write sign their cards represented having sex. Everyone standing put themselves at risk of getting HIV by exchanging names with the teacher or someone the teacher had exchanged names with and so on.

■ **Tell the student with the "C" card to sit down.** Tell the class that this student had a C on their card which means they always used a condom.

■ **Ask your students to notice that one person did not stand up.** The reason this student did not stand is because he or she was instructed not to allow anyone to record their name on their card. He or she was playing the role of someone who is abstinent.

<u>**Discussion:**</u> 15 minutes

■ **Ask:** How many people did the one HIV positive person potentially infect? Are they surprised?

■ **Ask:** Is it hard to use a condom all the time? What problems may develop?

■ **Ask:** In real life how does it feel to be someone who does not have sex? Do people give them a hard time?

■ **The teacher or facilitator should stress that in this game, you (the teacher) were in control of what role students would play. In reality, *they* are in control and responsible for the decisions they make.**

Think About It:

To me, a "date is" _____

_____

_____

_____

_____

For me, respecting myself on a date means _____

_____

_____

_____

_____

My definition of a "healthy relationship" is _____

_____

_____

_____

_____

I would break up with someone if _____

_____

_____

_____

_____

Chapter 8
Options After Care

Options After Care: Why This Chapter Matters

An important step to succeeding after you leave foster care is having a plan. That means knowing where you will live, as well as the first steps you will take to build a career.

This chapter explores options for life after care. Former foster youth write about the career and educational paths they chose when they left foster care. Princess Carr writes about cooking school. Matthew Dedewo explains why he joined the military. Tamecka Crawford describes her first few years in college. Mary n Podrazik describes the struggle to support herself on low-paying jobs without a college degree or job training.

You'll also find practical tips to help set you on the road to your dreams: information on getting a green card, applying for college and financial aid, and finding an internship.

Consider this chapter a map of possibilities for life after foster care. Which route you'll choose, of course, is entirely up to you.

Planning for the Long Run

There's a difference between having a job and having a career. A job is doing something just for the money. A career is doing something you enjoy.

Princess Carr

Scraping By

Working 'til I dropped paid off.

By MARY HANSON

About 20 years ago, I was a good-looking, small-figured 15-year-old young lady with freckles and brown hair. I was as naïve as the next person, seeking love to fill the gaping hole in my heart, and trying to get control over my life and find some direction.

I'd been in foster care since I was 3, and after moving from family to family, I was living in a group home that I hated. So when my caseworker offered to let me sign myself out of foster care and fly to Houston, Texas, to live with an aunt I'd never met, I agreed.

Alone in the World

I was desperate to get out of foster care. I wanted to make my own choices, and to have no one to blame for my decisions but myself. But I never felt so alone as the day when my social worker took me to the airport and put me on a plane to Texas to live with my aunt.

I was driven to succeed by an internal rage that had built up over years of being put down.

My aunt was high and argumentative when she picked me up at the airport. She looked as if she hadn't taken a shower. She stood in the baggage claim, smoking a cigarette. As soon as I got in her beat up silver Chevy Impala, my aunt lit a joint and handed it to me, trying to break the ice. I didn't know what else to do but take a hit and pass it back. I decided I should try to fit in until I figured out what else to do.

I thought my aunt would take care of me, or at least act like she cared a little, but that didn't happen. I had to sleep on a mattress on the floor of the living room, with no privacy. Even though New York state paid her a token amount to care for me, I was expected to pay for my own clothes, food, medical care and transportation.

I still remember my aunt getting angry because I drank all the milk.

"Damn, who drank the milk? Goddamnit, why do I have to buy all the groceries?" I felt so pitiful and helpless I wanted to cry. I felt alone in the world, stuck in a large city where I did not know my way around.

Getting Back to Me

It was a good thing I had saved money while I was working in New York State. That let me open a savings account and deposit the money. The next thing I did was panic. I had no job, no love, no friends, and no way to get back to New York. For the rest of the summer, I just tried to fit in, smoking pot and drinking even though I didn't want to. More than anything, I wanted to get away from my aunt and cousin and find a way to live on my own.

I knew that my life didn't have to be like this. For eight years I had lived with a stable foster family who showed me some basics about what a "normal" routine or family life could be like. My foster dad's government job gave him stability and a predictable dinnertime every evening. We dressed up to go out and dressed up for church on Sunday.

We were taught that lying was wrong, that you must groom yourself and be clean, have manners and be disciplined. They gave me some core values that, as I got to be an adult, stayed with me and guided me toward getting what I wanted out of life.

Proving Everyone Wrong

I knew it would not be easy to get out of my aunt's house and make it on my own. But I decided that I would do anything to survive. I'd have to find a boyfriend in Texas so I wouldn't be lonely, get a job that could support me, buy a car and graduate from high school.

Before age 15, I never had a choice about where to live or a say in any decisions that affected my life. Living with my aunt, I realized I did have the power to make my own choices. I was also driven to succeed by an internal rage that had built up over years of being put down by foster families and caseworkers who told me I'd never be more than a foster child. I wanted to prove everybody wrong.

www.youthcomm.org

When school started, my aunt put me in the work program instead of the college track. It was definitely not what I envisioned for myself. I attended school from 8 a.m. to 11 a.m. and went to work from noon to 9 p.m. I took no college prep courses, but I learned that I wanted more for myself than the low-paying, dead-end jobs everyone seemed to think I was suited for.

Fired From My First Job

I took my first job at Godfather's Pizza, but my aunt called and said, "Hey Murnie, I'm coming by to get a large supreme pizza in half an hour." That was her way of saying I owed her for letting me stay with her. I didn't know what to do. So I gave her the pizza—and the manager fired me.

In desperation, I applied for a job at Fayva Shoes and was hired. Most of my paychecks went to saving for a car, taxi rides to and from work, and the five dollars a day I had budgeted for food. I lost 13 pounds in one year because I could not afford to eat and was upset and anxious.

> **I figured that if I did everything physically possible, I was bound to succeed.**

Hard Choices

The next year, I knew I didn't want to be in retail, so I switched to the school's office work program, which I found more challenging and rewarding. I needed to learn how to type, so I went to my aunt's job late at night and practiced typing for hours.

I also started dating a guy named Kyle because I needed love and a companion, someone to talk to who understood me and cared about me. My boyfriend basically took over the parenting role and he also took me to and from work. He helped me and we fell in love, but he hurt me, too. When he drank, his personality changed and he'd verbally abuse me, never apologizing. I would cry and think about my foster care experiences. I couldn't cope with how hysterical I felt after those episodes.

When I was 18, he asked me to marry him and I said no. I wanted to be loved, but I knew it was not a healthy relationship. I wanted to spread my wings and discover who I was. My choice not to marry a man I loved was one of the hardest choices I've ever made in my life.

I graduated high school in the bottom five percent of my class, but I graduated. School was not paying me, so I skimmed by, never studying. I did not have the money or the grades to go to college so I decided to work a full-time job and a part-time job to try to get ahead.

Then my aunt started charging me $220 rent, so I moved into an apartment with a roommate. After two years of working and saving I was finally able to afford to start college. I signed up for an English class at the community college.

Far Behind in School

I was depressed when I started taking college classes because I needed remedial help. I never realized during high school that low grades, poor study habits and easy classes would haunt me. College was harder than I'd thought, but I didn't want to spend too much time studying, because then I'd have to work less, and I needed the money.

When I realized how far behind I was, I decided I would slowly bring my grade point average up by taking one class at a time. My grades came up to C's from D's, then to B's, and now I get A's. I learned to spend a lot of time studying, sacrificing some money I might make working in order to do well.

Through my high school work program, I'd been working as a file clerk and proofreader at Ace Appraisal, a real estate company. After two years, I was promoted to being the president's assistant. My goal was to continue school and become a real estate appraiser, which is someone who decides how much homes are worth. I had experience doing fieldwork and research and writing reports. But my boss said, "You don't have a college degree and I will not let you be an appraiser," although a degree was not a requirement.

So I quit Ace Appraisal and got a job as an assistant appraiser. After a couple of months I realized that company was unethical, so I quit that, too. Fortunately, I found a job as an appraiser. I finally had the job I wanted, but I'd failed to realize that the long hours of a professional job consume your time, making it impossible to concentrate in school. I constantly dropped college classes, but continued, on and off, because I was determined to finish.

In the late 1980s, the real estate market crashed and my problem was solved. Since I had little experience and little education, I was the first person to be laid off. When I lost my job, I took an easy 8 to 5 receptionist job because it was the only job I could get. I took a huge cut in pay and went back to school part-time.

During all those years, I worked 70 hours in a week, volunteering when the boss needed someone to help out, and using every waking moment of my day constructively. I only stopped when I was too physically exhausted to go anymore.

I had no confidence, but I knew no one cared about me but me, so I told myself that nothing would stop me. I was always scared of the future; fear and anger were the sole emotions that drove me to success. All I had was perseverance. I figured that if I did everything physically possible, I was bound to succeed. I was too anxious and scared of failing to stop working.

Building the Life I Dreamed About

Eventually, I did succeed. I became a real estate appraiser, and I had a good career. Five years ago, I got married, and my husband and I have built the life that I once could only dream about.

In some ways, though, I am still playing catch up. At 36, I am a junior in college, working on a bachelor's degree in psychology at the University of Wyoming, where we recently moved from Houston.

But for right now, I'm more a mother than a student. We have two toddlers, and because my husband is a surgeon, I'm able to stay home with them and spend time taking them to dance lessons, to go skating and to the park. I give them the love and attention every child deserves but I never got myself.

You're
LEAVING
care...

what's NEXT

?

Start

WANT a GOOD paying JOB?

if NO...

START work Now

Read "Scraping By," p. 246

if YES

want more stuff?
need more money?

Interested IN COLLEGE?

"YES"

Yes

Read "From 'Group Home Child' to College Success!" p. 270

No

Like working with your hands?

Like UNIFORMS and Push-ups?

Read "Job Corps: Train to Gain," p. 252

Read "Anchors Aweigh!" p. 263

STUDY

YES

TRADE SCHOOL

COLLEGE

Military

CAREER!

READY for College now?

NO

Steady job

Karolina Zanieniesko

www.youthcomm.org

Train to Gain

School wasn't working for me, so I'm joining Job Corps.

By MARISSA HOEY

I wanted to get my high school diploma but school wasn't working for me. I can't sit in school all day. It's just boring to me. So my other option was to get a GED, but I'm too young to get a GED. I'm only 16, and in New York City, where I live, you can't take the test to get your GED until the year your class graduates.

Then I heard about Job Corps. Job Corps is a program created by the U.S. Department of Labor. It helps young people build careers. It's for just about anybody ages 16-24 who can legally work in the United States. In Job Corps, you live on a campus, kind of like in college, and get your GED, get job training and get paid for it. The Job Corps people said it's easier for group home kids because we're used to living with other people.

You get to pick the trade you learn, like auto mechanics, painting and plastering, computer technology and nursing. You can learn your trade either in 6 months or one year. In a year you learn more and make more money.

I'm going for business management, and I'm going to stay a year. I'm going to be on the campus in Buffalo, New York, but they have campuses all over the country. I leave in two days. I'm nervous, but I know a few people who did Job Corps. They said it would be good for me because it gets you off the street and when you're on the campus you have nothing to concentrate on except the program.

One of the best things about Job Corps is that I'll still be in foster care while I do it. So when I'm through with my year there I can come back and go into an independent living program. When I do return, I plan to work part-time and also apply to college then. Job Corps will help me find a job and a college to attend. When you have Job Corps on your resume, I hear it's easy to get hired.

I know Job Corps is going to be more of an experience than being out here in the group home, 'cause now I'm not going to school and I'm not following curfew. In Job Corps, since you live on campus, there is no such thing as a curfew!

My biggest fear is messing up and getting kicked off the campus. One screw up, they can kick you out and you can't reapply. Still, I think it'll be good for me. I think it'll be a challenge.

—For more information call 1-800-733-JOBS, or go to the website: www.jobcorps.org.

Thinking Ahead

Working in fast food is a beginning, not a career.

By CHARLENE CARTER

Kelly is 24 and works at a fast food restaurant. She started working in fast food when she was living in foster care. At age 15, she got her

Charlene Carter

working papers, and after school and during summer break she would work at minimum wage jobs in fast food restaurants, clothing stores, local drug stores or movie theaters. Now, nine years later, she is still in this line of work.

While she was in foster care, that fast food salary seemed like a lot of money—she could buy clothes and CDs with it. But now that she has to pay her rent and transportation fees and buy food herself, that low salary is often not enough. And Kelly has no other financial support to fall back on in case of an emergency. She does not have the support of her biological family, and her old foster care agency can no longer help her financially. The money she makes helps her scrape by, but it does not give her the stability she needs.

So Kelly has to live using any means necessary. Instead of living in a decent-sized apartment, she rents a room. Instead of getting cable and a telephone hooked up, she just has a single 19-inch television and a boom box to keep her company. Kelly believes that if she had known how difficult it would be to survive on the salary she gets, she would have focused on developing skills in areas that paid better than fast food joints or movie theatres.

Minimum Wage Blues

Many foster care kids end up in Kelly's situation. While they live in foster care, they work at minimum wage jobs for extra money. Some figure they have all the time in the world to get training for a better job. And when you don't have to pay for your rent or food, the money from a low-paying job can seem like a lot. It can be spent (sometimes foolishly) on that special pair of blue jeans that cost $100 and the weekend at a concert. Having money makes you feel important because you can afford things.

But after foster youth leave the system, often, like Kelly, they find that it's hard to support themselves on minimum wage. And since the only work skills some teens living in foster care have involve fast food joints, that's where too many former foster kids get stuck working, even after they've left care and become adults.

Sure, minimum wage jobs can teach you a lot about being a good employee and help you develop positive work habits. And having that first job, no matter where it is, makes it easier to get the next one. So there's nothing wrong with working at a minimum wage job when you're a teen. But if those are the only skills we develop, it's not going to lead to salaries we can easily live on after we leave the system.

After foster youth leave the system, often, like Kelly, they find that it's hard to support themselves on minimum wage.

Kids in foster care should be encouraged to think more long term and take opportunities that will help them get higher paying jobs and have satisfying careers after they leave care. Many youth don't know that there are internships, volunteer opportunities and even paid jobs that can help them acquire the skills they need to get well-paying jobs after they leave the system.

Thinking Long Term

Some don't even realize how important it is to complete high school before you leave care. Having a GED or high school degree will enable you to be ready to start college or a degree program in an area that you are interested in. This may also allow you to choose from more jobs that pay well. Also, working in a company from the bottom, where there is a possibility of being promoted to a higher level, will place you in a position where you will have the potential to grow.

I talked to some former and current foster kids who found good-paying jobs, and most of them built up their skills working at internships and going to college before they found their jobs. Lishoné Bowsky, who has worked as an administrative assistant at a public relations company, built up her skills at many unpaid or low paid internships. She worked at record labels and completed a two year degree program in communications. These experiences allowed Lishoné to learn more about fields that she might be interested in, meet people who could give her a good recommendation to potential employers, and helped her become a controlled, responsible worker.

Max Moran, who has aged out of care now, has his MSW and is working at as a social worker. In high school, he had an internship where he was allowed to miss alternate weeks at school to intern in a field he was interested in—social work. That helped him start laying the foundation for a career when he left the system.

Making Contacts

To find out what field you might be interested in, think about what you enjoy doing. If you like to cook, you might want to be a chef. If you like reading, writing and arguing, you might want to become a lawyer. Then talk to the adults in your life about the field you're interested in. See if they know someone who is already working in that field who could explain how you could get experience in that line of work. See if they know of internships or other opportunities that might be open to you.

There's nothing wrong starting your career at Mickey D's. The thing is not to let that be the end of the road for you. So set your hopes high and start developing the skills you need to make it on your own after you leave care.

How to Find an Internship

By CHARLENE CARTER

Internships are short-term jobs that usually last about two or three months, and are geared towards helping young people learn about a specific job or business. They can give you the chance to see what a profession will really be like.

Charlene Carter

For instance, if you are interested in the advertising business, you might be an intern at an advertising agency, where you would see firsthand a little about how the business works and what types of jobs you might be interested in.

Internships are mainly for young people, so it's good to take advantage of them while you're young. At some internships, you're matched with a mentor who can help provide you with some support and guidance. Some internships are paid, others are not. When you are looking for an internship, here are some handy tips that can help you land one that's right for you:

1. Start Early.
Don't wait until the end of the school year to apply for a summer internship. Some summer internship programs start hiring as early as November for the following summer.

2. Work with Your Counselors.
Youths in foster care have many counselors. There is the school counselor, the social worker, the educational vocational counselor and the child care worker. Oftentimes when our personal resources are used up, someone else has resources that we would be interested in. So it is important to talk with the adults in your life to see if they know of opportunities you might be interested in.

3. Research.
Talking to adults you know is the best start, but you can also branch out: Ask librarians where you can look for internships and find out about youth employment services in your area.

4. Be Informed. Find out what qualifications you need, what the application procedure is, and what your duties and responsibilities will be. These facts will help you decide if the internship is right for you.

5. Apply for the Internship. You may need a lot of material for this: school transcripts, phone numbers of people who can talk about you as a worker, an application and a resume. Make sure you meet the deadline.

6. Interview. Many internships require you to interview for the job. For your interview, be on time. Dress neatly. Don't chew gum. Look the person who's interviewing you in the eye. If you have questions about the internship, now is the time to ask them.

7. Start Your Internship. Learn as much as you can, and treat it like a job, even if you're not being paid. You'll get a good recommendation (which is worth a lot by itself). And you'd be amazed how many internships eventually turn into paid jobs.

Cooking Up a Future

I need book smarts and confidence
to become a chef.

By PRINCESS CARR

One day last August, when I was lying around doing nothing, I saw an ad on TV for the New York Restaurant School. It showed students and teachers in the kitchen making things and smiling. It gave me an excited feeling. I wanted to be one of them.

Princess Carr

For years I'd wanted to go to cooking school to be a chef. I love cooking, especially since there is no wrong or right when you are making up your own dishes. I usually don't use recipes, unless I have never made the dish before or I am trying to impress someone. Nine times out of 10, if it tastes good while you are preparing it, it's not going to come out tasting bad.

Cooking Gave Me Peace

My mother started to teach me to cook when I was 5 years old. She started with the basics, like rice and eggs and pancakes. As I got older, she showed me how to clean and fry chicken, and make mashed potatoes and corn bread. Cooking wasn't a chore to me, it was fun. I liked that my mom thought I was big enough to cook all by myself.

> **It took me years to understand that you have to do things you don't want to do to get what you want.**

When I moved into the system, the group home staff found out that I could cook, so I was always put on kitchen duty. Most of the time I was alone in the kitchen. I liked the peace of doing something on my own without being bothered. (And when I cooked, I didn't have to help clean up.)

Now when I'm upset, I cook. When I cook I feel nothing, I hear nothing, and I pay attention only to what I am doing. I feel much better when my dish is done and I can eat.

College Material?

I also had always wanted to go to college but never thought I would really get there. As a child, I never had a problem with learning, but I could not sit through an eight-hour school day.

As a teenager, I didn't make it through the ninth grade, because my home life caught up with me and turned everything into one major disaster. I stopped going to school altogether.

People called me stupid and said I'd grow up to be nothing, and part of me believed them. I started thinking that I was a lost soul, someone to feel sorry for, so it was OK not to do anything with my life.

But another part of me hoped that, somehow, I would make it and be a success. When I turned 16, I decided to take my GED so that when I was ready to go back to school, I could. I was scared that I would fail, but not really surprised when I passed with a far higher score than I needed.

Going for My Degree

When I saw that ad on TV, I decided to enroll at the New York Restaurant School. I called the school and spoke to a very nice man who made me feel good about my decision. Then I went down to the school and enrolled. I had to fill out an application, write an essay and speak to the financial aid people. I did it all in one day.

I found out I have to pay tens of thousands of dollars in tuition. But I got financial aid and a loan. You might understand how stressed it made me feel to take out a loan. But I still think it'll be better for me in the future to take out the loan and go. I can pay it back when I get my degree and a job.

In October, I started school. My program is Culinary Arts and Restaurant Management. That's a two-year program. I go to school five nights a week, from 6 p.m. to 11 p.m.

Book Smarts

I chose this school because I love to cook, but in reality, restaurant school is all about being careful, and learning the basics. We spent weeks learning to handle knives. I had to learn all about fractions, which I hate, because I'm bad at math. And we learned things like how to keep food fresh, why certain foods go bad faster than others, and what kinds of diseases you can get from food.

I spend so much time learning from books that I start to get antsy. Homework has never been easy for me, and to be honest, reading all the textbooks is a bore. I won't cook until the third semester. I can't really say that I'm happy about that, but I did know it before I signed up.

I try to remind myself that my pain is not in vain. I am learning things, and I am setting myself up for a job I'll enjoy. It took me years to understand that you have to do things you don't want to do to get what you do want. This is just one of those times for me.

One day in class I got two assignments back: an A and a D-. That D- broke my heart and my faith in myself. I started to cry. I could not believe that I had gotten such a low grade on something I worked hard on. And I felt afraid, because I want to succeed but I'm afraid I won't.

'Don't Give Up'

The teacher said I could re-do the assignment, but I kept crying. I felt so stupid. I knew that my teacher was really concerned and really scared. I could see these feelings in her face and I could hear them in her voice as she kept calling my name over and over.

But I could not answer her because I felt like my world had fallen down around me because of one bad grade. I was ready to give up right then and there. Then a guy in my class said to me, "You're just looking for a reason to give up. Just do your best, that's all."

I did not feel better right away after that, but I did feel grateful for what he said. He seemed to know that I want to do well but am scared.

Taking a Break

Still, not long after that, I took a break from school to get my life together. When I started my classes, I was living with my girlfriend, but we started having problems and I had to move out. I knew I'd fail my classes if I stayed in school, because I had to go to a homeless shelter, and all that was too much stress to get through at once.

I figured that when I started again, at least I'd know what to expect. I told myself, "I'm not giving up, even though I am giving in to my feelings right now. My heart needs time to mourn." I had faith in myself that I'd return, but I was also afraid I might not.

When spring semester came, though, I enrolled all over again. I'm still living in a shelter, but I believe I can get through the semester this time.

I Need to Let My Fear Go

I have never wanted to succeed at something as much as I want to succeed at cooking school. Sometimes I believe that all I can do is fail. Other times I believe that I can do anything that I put my mind to. I feel like how well I do in cooking school will tell me who is right about me.

I know that if I really want to succeed I'll have to let my fear go and try as hard as I can. I hope I can do that. I want to do something that I can be proud of.

Anchors Aweigh!

I knew I'd look good in Navy blues.

By MATTHEW DEDEWO

I joined the Navy because I wanted to feel the thrill of combat. I wanted to travel and be a part of something everyone respected. I also

Matthew Dedewo

wanted the perks you can get from giving a few years of service—a college scholarship, medical benefits and a better shot at getting most government jobs. But mostly, I wanted to prove to myself that I could make it through boot camp.

Boot camp, or basic training, is where you're taught survival skills and how to act in the military. You also get physically trained. Though I'd seen boot camp in the movies, I had no idea what I was really getting into.

I Failed the First Drug Test

I had decided to join the Navy branch because I love the water and their uniforms. (Blue and white are my favorite colors and I knew I would look good in them.) To join the Army or Navy you have to be 18, or 17 with a high school diploma or GED. You also have to pass some tests, like drug and alcohol tests as well as some written ones, like in school.

For most of the branches of the military, it's OK if you've been in trouble with the law, or have used drugs in the past as long as it's not in your system when you take the test. I smoked weed, but I thought it would be out of my system by the time I took the test. It wasn't. I failed and had to wait six months before I could take the test again. That time I passed.

On the Plane to Boot Camp

I was 23 when I finally boarded the plane to boot camp. It was the middle of January when I landed in Chicago's O'Hare airport with the other Navy recruits from New York.

On the bus to the Recruit Training Center, I looked through the frosty window and saw divisions marching by. They were all dressed the same, wearing their blue uniforms with combat boots. No one looked too jolly. There was no laughing, no joking around, and definitely no lagging behind.

I found it hard to hold my face together when one of the thugs among us got yelled at for not walking straight as we made our way to the base. When all of us had to call out the single digits of our social security numbers, one girl kept saying "nineteen" instead of "one" and "nine." She got screamed at badly.

I quickly learned that I needed to listen carefully to what I was asked to do and then do just that. Otherwise, I would get screamed at or forced to do push-ups until my toes ached.

Everyone was issued military clothing, sneakers and boots. Everything we came in with, down to our drawers, was put in a box and mailed to our homes.

In the Navy there are five different uniforms and they had to be placed in the lockers a certain way. Our metal bunk beds had to be made a certain way in a certain amount of time. Uniforms had to be folded and worn properly, and all these things were inspected. Even our underwear had to be folded right.

> **I quickly learned that I needed to listen carefully to what I was asked to do and then do just that.**

Folding Underwear Like Sissies

One day after classes we found half the beds flipped over and most of the lockers emptied and turned upside down. It seemed that there was a surprise inspection and we had failed miserably. We had thought we were going to be firing rifles, jumping out of planes and playing war games. Instead, we were folding underwear like a bunch of sissies. But I started to understand why the officers were so tough on us recruits. They got on us about every little thing because out in the fleet any little detail you overlook could cost you your life and the lives of those around you.

Those first few days, while they drilled all the rules and ways of Navy life into us recruits, we didn't get a chance to sleep. Our day began at 5 in the morning and lights out was at 10. It was exhausting. Some of us learned how to sleep while standing.

We were bombarded with physical and medical tests to make sure we were able to handle what lay ahead. When the tests came back, three guys who got high in the hotel the night before the tests were sent home with dishonorable discharges.

Because I had a GED instead of a high school diploma, I was placed in a special division where I had to spend 10 weeks in boot camp instead of eight like everyone who had a high school diploma. Our division was thought of as troublemakers because we didn't have the patience to last through high school. Also, some of us had either used drugs or been in trouble with the law.

To the frustration of the officers overseeing us, we lived up to that reputation. When we got sent to self-esteem and anger management classes, we were all pissed off and swore we didn't need them.

Getting Pumped?

Some of our days were spent practicing marching formations, but the majority were spent in classes. We had two chances to pass the test of each week or we got "washed back." At first I couldn't believe it. If I had wanted an education I would've just gone back to college. I wanted to get pumped and blow stuff up, not sit and study. But I began to understand that being mentally prepared was perhaps a human's best ammunition.

That's not to say we didn't do a lot of physical work. We did. We often ran first thing in the morning. There were three physical training phases that we had to pass, or get washed back. First we had to run about a mile and a half in less than 12 minutes, and we weren't allowed to stop once we started. I started out at a good pace, but by the third lap I was out of breath and my legs felt like they were going to pop. I wanted to stop and ask for a glass of lemonade, but I was determined to not spend an extra week in boot camp. I made it.

I realized for the first time that running fast was not a matter of strength or energy, but of will power. I saw that my mind had more power than I thought.

On Sundays we were allowed go to the church on base or write letters and study. But no sleeping. If anyone was caught sleeping they got a penalty. Too many penalties got a person washed back to a group of recruits that was a week or two behind them. That meant more time in boot camp.

I Hit a Navy Seal

In week three we learned how to swim. We had to jump off a 20 foot high platform into a deep pool and swim to the edge. I was one of the cocky recruits who lied about knowing how to swim. I said I could swim "a little bit." But really, the only way I could move in the water was if I walked along the bottom.

When I jumped off the platform into the pool and didn't feel my feet hit the bottom, I panicked. I started flapping my arms frantically and hit one of the Navy Seals (they were our instructors for that phase) in the head. He pulled me out of the water and I got away with only a lecture. (That was a lot less painful than what I had expected.) Not everyone can say that they smacked a Navy Seal in the head.

Soon, I knew what would get me in trouble and what wouldn't. That made me a little more sure about myself and the days started to fly by. I started looking forward to the runs and reading my manuals on Sundays instead of lounging. I also started feeling confident about doing "watch," which is where you guard a post for two or four hours and challenge everyone who comes near it.

In week six, after we had enough practice shooting at moving targets, we were allowed to let loose and have some fun at Captain's Cup. It's a one day event where divisions compete against each other in physical feats like running, swimming, push-ups and sit-ups. Our division would've won but we had team leaders who were real knuckleheads and couldn't lead a river downstream. I think our officers purposely did that to test our patience and get us in the habit of taking orders from people who piss us off.

Stuck in a Gas Chamber

In week seven, we learned about lifesaving techniques, tools and gas masks. We also had the pleasure of spending a few minutes in a chamber filled with tear gas. We thought we were tough and could handle it, but we were crying with our noses dripping and drool coming out of our mouths. It felt like my eyes, nose and lungs were burning up, but I managed to crack a smile when a section leader (a short, cocky guy who no one liked) panicked and tried to run out of the chamber.

In week eight came Battle Stations. A loud siren and whistles blowing woke us in the middle of the night. The lights were blinking off and on, and a loud threatening voice told us that we had 10 seconds to get our gear on. Until the following morning, we had to do everything as if our lives depended on it. There were six tests set up for us, all at different locations on base. In one, we had to race through a battlefield getting casualties to safety without getting shot. It was a night I'll never forget.

At 8 the next morning we got a congratulatory speech from the officer-in-charge. It was graduation day. It felt good to hear. We had proven ourselves to be worthy enough to protect our country. People's families and friends came to witness our graduation ceremony.

I had no one to invite but I had become so close with my division that it wasn't a problem. Two months ago we were at each other's necks. Now everyone was introducing mothers and fathers. We took pictures of ourselves holding each other's kids.

Hello to a New Me

Boot camp was just the beginning of military life, but it was an important part. It was like giving birth to a new me. I had always been disciplined and respectful, but now I knew how to discipline my mind and body. Before boot camp I could hardly run three blocks before stopping to catch my breath. Now I could run 3 ½ miles in under twenty minutes.

I became more focused and I learned not to panic despite the situation. I also found people I could count on in an emergency. I made friends who I stayed in contact with even after some of them got stationed overseas. I feel like those qualities will help me a lot, hopefully for the rest of my life.

Carded

I need my green card to go to college or get a job.

By MERLI DESROSIER

One day I went to Bed Bath & Beyond for a job interview. I was so nervous and scared because I really needed the job. That same day I found out that I did get the job, but I couldn't start working until I could prove I was legally able to work in this country.

Merli Desrosier

I'm not a United States citizen and I don't have a green card, which lets immigrants work legally in the U.S. My father and mother are from Haiti. I was born in Belgium, Europe. When I was 3 months old, my parents brought me with them to the U.S., where I've lived ever since. But because I'm not a citizen and I don't have a green card, I can't vote, work, or receive financial aid from the government for college.

Now it's a major stress for me. I'm 17. I'm getting close to aging out of foster care and I don't have a way to work legally. I don't know how I'm going to support myself or pay for college without the aid of the government. Also—though I don't have to worry about this—without your green card, if you get in trouble with the law, even for a small thing, that can mean serious problems for you. In some cases you can be sent back to the country you came from.

It turns out I'm not the only young person in foster care who's having problems getting my citizenship papers. When I went to the Door, a center for New York City teens, and spoke to a lawyer named Monica de la Torre about my problem, she told me that she deals with about 100 foster youth every year who are immigrants and need help getting a green card. Luckily, there's a special law that allows foster teens in the United States to get a green card. "You can only file through this law if you are in foster care," said de la Torre.

www.youthcomm.org

Foster Youth Eligible for Cards

But too often, caseworkers aren't aware of this law. Sometimes they don't even know when a teen on their caseload is an immigrant. A lot of times they don't think to ask young people about their legal status until the teen needs to find a job or apply for financial aid.

If you need a green card, be sure to talk with your caseworker and law guardian about it early on, because it can take as long as a year to be approved for one. But once you submit your application, even if you haven't received your green card yet, you may be able to get permission to work after 90 days. One day, when you do receive your green card in the mail, you'll be able to sigh, because now you can get a job, get the government to help you pay for college and last, but definitely important, you'll eventually be able to become an American citizen.

From 'Group Home Child' to College Success

By TAMECKA L. CRAWFORD

Going off to college for the first time can be a scary experience for anyone, but especially for a foster child. We don't have the support of a parent, and a lot of times we feel as if we're alone in the world. Before I left for Sullivan County Community College in New York state, I started to wonder what college life would be like for me.

Although I wanted so badly to be independent, I still wanted someone there to fall back on. How would I survive all alone in a strange place? Could I make it as a college student? Would I fail or drop out? I worried about people finding out I had lived in a group home and treating me differently or making fun of me. I even wondered if my professors would treat me differently.

First Day Nerves

When I first started classes, things seemed fine. I had six classes and the workload was all right. But after a little while I met a guy and started spending lots of time with him, skipping classes and not studying. I started having trouble, and my grades dropped tremendously in history and math. I told myself I had all the time in the world to pull them up.

I found myself using the excuse of being in foster care every time I missed a class or failed an exam. A lot of times I would say to myself, "Oh, I'm in a group home. Who cares if I go to class or not, or if I failed an exam or even if I passed one?"

'Group Home Child'

I felt as if the words "group home child" were hanging over my head. Even though nobody treated me differently, in the back of my mind I imagined they were. Like at the Bursar's window (the place that deals with your bills), I felt that they were hesitant to deal with me because they knew I was in foster care.

My self-esteem was very low my first semester. I sometimes just gave up and didn't care. As a result, I completed my first semester with a 1.0 grade point average (like a D average), and ended up on academic probation.

I felt nobody cared for me. And it showed. I felt this way because I didn't have any family support. I kept making the mistake of comparing my life to students who had parents calling often, and coming to visit them. They also used to get care packages filled with all sorts of things, including their favorite foods, money, and supplies they asked for.

> **I found myself using the excuse of being in foster care every time I missed a class or failed an exam.**

Wanting Family

I wanted so badly to have someone care about me like that. I felt neglected and jealous.

I remember hearing my roommate talk on the phone with her mother, describing what classes she liked more than others. I wished so badly that could be my mother or somebody who really cared for me. Although I did stay in contact with people from my former group home, it wasn't a substitute for family.

Just before the end of the first semester I realized that I had wasted time feeling sorry for myself and I had to do something about it. I never thought the semester would go so quickly. Like I said before, when you first get to college you think you have all this time, then before you know it, it's over.

Gradually I realized that time was passing me by and nobody was going to care for me until I cared for myself. I was so wrapped up in worrying about having people do things for me and care for me that I wasn't taking the time to care for myself.

I got tired of using the fact that I was in foster care as an excuse. I was tired of failing my exams. I was tired of crying. At the same time, I also noticed that the people who I was envying weren't doing so well in their classes either.

www.youthcomm.org

Tired of Excuses

I finally realized it wasn't because I was in foster care that I was failing my classes. It was because I had been paying too much attention to what people thought of me and how they treated me, and too little attention to my schoolwork. I had to accept the fact that I was in foster care and move on. It wasn't being in foster care holding me back, it was me holding myself back.

It was right after spring break that I decided to wipe my eyes and find ways to start my independent life. The first thing I decided to do was to attend all my classes Monday morning and start pulling my grades up.

In my second semester my grade point average shot up to 3.25. I was studying night and day, especially subjects like history, which I always had problems with. I went to a tutor who worked with me and I also found other college students who were good in a particular subject to help me. In exchange, I'd type a paper for them or make them dinner.

I started letting professors know I was having problems and some of them would meet with me privately to help me. Or if they saw that I was making an effort they would let me know, by saying, "I see that your grades are dropping again. Are you having trouble studying?" Some of them would give me methods or extra material to use.

Help From a Counselor

My next step was to get counseling. When you're on academic probation you automatically get group counseling. I'd had counseling in the group home, but I never liked it because I felt we were pre-judged. But in college I felt it would help to have a one-on-one counselor because I realized I needed help dealing with the transition from the group home to college life.

I had a nice female counselor who listened to me talk about school, my group homes, and other things on my mind. At the end of the sessions she would give suggestions on how to deal with my problems. It helped me realize that while I couldn't have the family relationships that I wanted so badly, I could thank God for the people who were taking the time out to help me any way they could.

I also got a part-time job to make some extra money when the group home couldn't help me pay for whatever I needed. I was even able to put some money in the bank for rainy days. Basically, I started trying not to depend on the system too much.

Through counseling, I realized that in some ways being a foster child was an advantage for me.

Strength From Foster Care

For example, living in a group home was a big help in adjusting to college life because I had already learned how to live with different people's personalities and attitudes. Also, I had already learned a sense of independence. Just like in a group home, when you're in college you have to do things for yourself and make sure things are getting done to help you.

But one thing that was easier for me about the group home was that everyone has something in common: our family couldn't or wouldn't take care of us. We all understood that and could talk about it amongst each other. But in college I met people from all sorts of different backgrounds, and sometimes I felt envious of their lifestyles. When other students were planning their spring breaks in Hawaii or Virginia, I was deciding on what movie I was going to see during the break, or whether to go visit a relative or stay in the group home. Sometimes I would just end up at the group home the entire time.

I learned that in order for anything to change, I first must care about myself. Then I'll be able to care about the situation and do what I need to. I'm looking forward to finishing my last semester. My overall grade point average is 3.0, which is great compared to how things were looking the end of my first semester.

The Real Deal about Applying to College

By DEBRA SAMUELS

My fears about applying to college were due to misconceptions and a lack of information. Here are some common questions you might have and some helpful answers based on responses from the Options Center, a college counseling program in Manhattan.

What should I do first?

Answer: Trying to decide what school to attend and how to go about applying is very hard to do without help, so the most important first step is getting that help.

Get a copy of your high school transcript near the end of your junior year in high school. Then, talk to a college counselor in school or at your agency, or go to a counseling program outside of school.

Should I stay close to home or go away to college?

Answer: For foster youth, this is a complicated question. Where is your home? Will it remain there for you during four years of college? For example, you may worry that if you go away to school you won't have any place to go during vacations and holidays. Talk to your social worker or counselor about these questions.

You shouldn't go away to college just because you are running away from a difficult situation at home. You should have positive reasons for wanting to go away to college.

Also, adjusting to a new environment away from home can be difficult. That's why it's important to visit schools before you attend.

www.youthcomm.org

How important is the S.A.T.?

Answer: It is important to take the S.A.T. if you're going to a school that requires it. (Many colleges do, but most community colleges don't.) But the S.A.T. isn't the only thing the colleges look at.

Grades and courses are far more important than the S.A.T. The personal essay, an interview, and your grades can possibly make up for a low S.A.T. score. Each college looks at these things differently, so it's important for you to know the requirements of the schools you're interested in.

Note: Most people in foster care will qualify for a "fee waiver," which means you don't have to pay to take the S.A.T. Ask your college counselor about the fee waiver. This will also qualify you for the college application fee waiver (see next page).

How can a young person in foster care pay for college?

Answer: Almost all young people in foster care will qualify for some form of financial aid. There are many types of loans, grants, and scholarships available. The best way to find out about financial aid is to contact one of the counseling programs in your area.

You should also apply to private schools as well as public schools. Private schools cost more, but they also have more money for scholarships and financial aid than public schools, which depend on state funding.

What about the financial aid forms?

Answer: The forms are tricky, because if you make one little error, such as leaving a blank, then they will be sent back to you for corrections. That's why seeking out help and applying for financial aid EARLY is the best advice. If the forms are sent in early enough—usually in January of the year you're going to college—there's enough time for corrections and meeting deadlines. After you've been accepted, call the college's financial aid office if you have questions or need help. Make an appointment to speak to one of the financial aid officers.

www.youthcomm.org

Isn't there a fee for applying to each school?

Answer: Yes, but you can find out how to get a "fee waiver" form from each college. This means you don't have to pay the application fee, which is usually between $30 and $50. A fee waiver itself costs nothing—it is just a form you fill out and send to the college.

Am I at a disadvantage in applying to college because I'm in foster care?

Answer: Absolutely not. Students in foster care are actually at a slight advantage over other students in several ways. The financial aid process is made simpler because you're considered a ward of the state and therefore financially independent. This means that the usual tax forms are not needed. (But you do have to watch the size of the loans you take out, especially if there's no family to back you up.)

Another advantage is that students in care often have better developed life skills and a sense of independence than the average college-bound student. Many foster care youth have had to learn how to take care of themselves in the system because no one else would. These skills will be important in college.

Two Things Not to Forget When Applying to College

By DEBRA SAMUELS

Let's face it, when it comes to filling out your college application, many foster youth are bound to be a bit nervous. I know I was. You'll be filling out applications for each school, financial aid forms and the other documents. But in the crush of all the paperwork, you'll also want to get recommendations and write your college essay (if the schools you're applying to require these.)

You may feel that you're not smart enough to go, or you may want to go and don't know where or how to start. Then there are those of us who start to apply and give up because we let the application process get us down. I had all of these fears but I overcame them, and you can too.

Now that I'll soon be entering my third year at college, I can look back at my senior year in high school and share some tips that might make the application process less frightening.

1. Get Recommendations. One thing that caused a

constant uproar among the seniors when I was applying to college was having to get teachers' recommendations. This was a hassle, because at the start of the school year many of our current teachers don't know us well enough to write a letter. This means hunting down teachers from years before, who usually don't remember us well enough to write pleasant things.

Thank goodness that I did some detective work and discovered that the letters weren't restricted to just teachers. Some schools asked for recommendations from just about anybody—friends of the family, or adult acquaintances as long as they knew you well and supported your application. So I used one from my music instructor and from the school counselor I was close to.

2. Write the Essay. The application is the place where you

begin convincing the schools that you are the student for them. If you didn't do too well on your S.A.T.'s and your grades are sort of borderline, the student essay that many colleges require can give your application that extra push.

The essay is an opportunity for you to make yourself stand out from among all the other applicants. You may not think there is anything interesting to write about yourself, but you'd be surprised. Anything that you do outside of your schoolwork is important to the colleges you are applying to. Colleges want to enroll students from many backgrounds with different experiences.

If you feel stuck or are convinced that there is nothing interesting about you, then ask around. You'd be surprised at what some people know about you that you don't even know yourself.

Another thing that can help is describing anything that has had an impact on your life. If you are in foster care, I'm sure you have pages to write on that topic. It doesn't have to be a sob story, just a brief description of an event that altered your life in some way.

Maybe you want to talk about how being in foster care has made you determined to achieve as many goals as possible, despite the odds that are against you. That's something that I chose to write about and it worked for me!

Activity Page for Group Leaders

Exploring Options for Life After Care

> **Topic:** Exploring options for life after care
>
> **Goal:** To help teens compare the benefits of college, the military, vocational school
>
> **Time:** 1 hour
>
> **Activity and reading story:** 30 minutes

■ **Have teens do the activity** "You're Leaving Care…What's Next?" on p. 251. Tell group they must all aim for a "career" or a "steady job" but note that there are different ways to get there.

■ **Read stories:** As students go through the flow chart, they will see instructions to read specific stories. Tell them to stop and read that story on the page number indicated.

They will read either "From 'Group Home Child' to College Success" on p. 270, "Anchors Aweigh!" on p. 263, which is about the military, or "Job Corps: Train to Gain" on p. 252.

Group Activity: 25 minutes

Reading: Divide teens into three groups based on the story they read. For instance, everyone who read "From 'Group Home Child' to College Success" should be in a group together.

Ideally, one group will have read the story on p. 270 about college. One will have read the story on p. 263 about the military. The third group will have read about Job Corps, on p. 252. However, you can also do the debate with any two of the groups.

Discussion: Tell groups to discuss the advantages of the program they read about, and write down the three best reasons why someone should attend the program (college, Job Corps, or the Navy).

Activity Page for Group Leaders

(continued)

Debate: 10-15 minutes

Tell groups that they are *recruitment officers* for the program they read about. For instance, if they read about Job Corps, it is their job to convince kids to go to Job Corps. If they read about the Navy, it is their job is to convince teens to join the Navy.

Pick one especially mature teen in the group (or use yourself) to be the "target" of the "recruiters." Tell groups that that teen (or yourself) is trying to choose what they will do after they leave foster care.

Give each group 2-3 minutes to try to convince the teen (or you) to attend their program. Have a small prize for the winning group—for instance chocolate kisses. Announce this prize in advance and put the kisses enticingly on display right in front of the recruit.

After groups have presented their arguments, have the teen (or yourself) ask each group two questions. Have teen (or yourself) choose the program whose team made the best argument.

Optional: Give each team a chance to rebut the arguments of the other teams. Then let each team respond. (This can get quite lively.)

Note: You (or the teen) have to be unbiased in picking the option that sounds best based on the *quality of the arguments* each team makes—not your personal preference.

Closing activity: 10 minutes

Explain to the group that they have learned about some serious options available to them after they leave foster care. Have each teen say, briefly, what option she or he is considering, and why.

Chapter 9
Making a Plan

Making a Plan:
Why This Chapter Matters

Congratulations! You're on the last chapter of the book, and we know you've learned a lot—you've learned about handling your money, finding and keeping a job, finding an apartment and keeping it clean, forming a support system, and taking good care of yourself physically and emotionally.

Now you're ready to make a plan for life after care. In the next few pages you'll hear from three successful former foster youth who made plans for leaving care and triumphed.

Learn how Giselle John, who today runs her own youth program, made a plan for leaving care, and the obstacles she had to overcome to stay on track. Xavier Reyes will tell you how you can set your own goals. And you'll find worksheets to help you do that. Don't forget to read Mario Drummonds' inspirational story about how he overcame his fears and his rules for success.

Congratulations, you're almost there!

The Day I Left Care

The birthday I aged out was on Friday the 13th. My roommate had already moved out and the agency was going to close down the apartment for us that day. I think I was a little bit depressed but then my friends called me up and said, "Hey, it's your birthday." They didn't really know that I was in foster care. They didn't know I had just been kicked out of my apartment with nowhere to live. But they were like, "We're going to go out and have fun for your birthday."

So I went out with my friends and woke up the next day on their couch where I stayed a good two or three (well, actually, five) months. I woke up on the couch and I never really left. They had just gotten the apartment and they needed another roommate so I was really happy. Things never happen quite the way you plan it, but it still helps to have a plan.

Lenny Jones

Countdown to Independence

By GISELLE JOHN

My next birthday is D-Day! No, this has nothing to do with World War II or other ancient history. It has to do with my future, with me leaving the system!

Giselle John

I know this day—the day I age out, emancipate, whatever you want to call it—has been coming for a long time, and I've been looking forward to it with longing and anxiety. I have planned and replanned everything about aging out, from budgeting my money to apartment hunting. This is not to say that I'm totally ready to be living on my own. In fact, I'm nervous about it! But I'm also confident that things will work out because I know I've planned well.

Laying the Groundwork

I began to lay the groundwork for the day I age out of the system when I was 19. I went to my independent living classes and got my first job, at Dress Barn. Then I opened a bank account so I could begin to save money for the day I would be living on my own.

Even though my job didn't pay much money (it was minimum wage) and constantly tested my patience, I considered it better than nothing. Many times I wanted to quit, but that's not how the real world runs. With this job I could save money for my future. And I knew I needed to do that.

One Year Left

To figure out how much money I should save by the time I left the system, I started budgeting how much I would spend each month on rent, food, phone, entertainment, transportation and clothes when I was on my own. (Very costly!)

When I turned 20, I had one full year of planning left before I aged out. (Unfortunately, foster youth in many states emancipate at 18. If that's the case for you, you have to do everything earlier than I did. Good Luck!) That's when I really started counting my time left in the system. I did some serious reevaluations. I asked myself questions like: Where do I want to live? How much rent can I afford to pay? How much money do I need to save? Do I want to share an apartment with a roommate?

I also started paying attention to how people who already had apartments of their own lived, and even how they furnished their homes. I was excited about decorating an apartment, but I knew I had to be realistic about money when buying furniture.

I began calculating how much money I could save in the time I had left. If I saved $50 per week until my birthday, I figured I'd have a decent amount of money. Plus, I'd get to add to it my discharge grant that I'll get when I age out, independent living stipends and scholarship money.

So I set a goal. I decided I wanted to have saved $5,000 by the time I was 21. For the months to come, reaching that goal became one of the main things I thought about. I was set on doing it no matter what. But I had no idea just how much determination it would take for me to reach it, and how many obstacles I was going to face. Saving money, it turns out, is not easy.

> **I decided I wanted to have saved $5,000 in total by the time I was 21.**

For one, because I work in a women's clothing store, I end up buying a lot of the clothes the store sells. Sometimes I literally work to pay my lay-away bills. Not to mention that there are so many other clothing stores in that area. I found myself spending a lot of my hard-earned money on clothes! Real self-control was needed here.

Eventually reality set in. I reminded myself that I had less than a year left before I would be paying for everything—clothes, rent, bills—on my own. I knew I needed to save for that. So I told myself, "That's it, I have to stop spending on things like clothes." It wasn't easy, and I didn't stop completely, but I did slow down a lot.

Eleven Months Left

I started college, and started learning just how hard it is to work and go to school. I still had my regular job, but now I had gotten work-study at school, which I took advantage of. Work study let me work on my college campus. So I worked between classes, then went to my regular job after school. I was busy…and tired.

Ten Months Left

Then a blessing came my way. I got financial aid, which helps students pay for college, and which really started me off on the road to saving. When you get financial aid—and just about everyone in foster care can get for it—the aid first pays your school for your tuition. Then, whatever money is left over goes to you.

After they finished paying my school for my tuition, $2300 was left over. I got $1,000 of it my first semester in school, and would get the second part the next semester. Some of that money I spent on books and school things. But since I was living in a foster home and not paying for rent or food, I also saved some of it. Instead of spending it all on new clothes (which I was tempted to do), I actually put it away for my birthday, emancipation day!

I put that money in the bank along with another $1,000 scholarship I won, plus $400 I'd gotten back from my former foster mother. Things were looking up.

Eight Months Left

And then things looked down again. I didn't squander my money, I just gave too much of it to people who needed it more than I did. If someone I knew was in need, I just gave them money. I felt like since I had money saved up, I needed to help those close to me. I temporarily forgot that the day would come when I'd really need that money to fall back on. During this time, I went from having $2,700 to only $1,000.

I realized, once again, that I had lost control and had to do something about it. I started a paid internship. It didn't pay much, but I was determined to save some of the money I'd make for aging out. I also knew that I would be getting more money back from school financial aid the next semester, so I felt like I was back on my feet again. I reshaped my budget plan. Now it looked like this:

$2,300—financial aid (total for both semesters)

$1,000—work

$320—independent living stipends for six months

$500—internship

$750—New York discharge grant, which I'd get when I aged out

A total of $4,850! But it was still short $250 to reach my goal of $5,000. And already I'd spent about half of my financial aid money on school supplies, clothes and giving to others. I wondered how I would ever reach my goal. I figured out different plans, like working more hours at Dress Barn or becoming a lifeguard as well. (I'm a good swimmer and in New York, lifeguarding pays around $8.50 an hour.) In the end, I got offered a better, higher-paying internship doing community planning.

Six Months Left

Six months before my 21st birthday, I filled out the housing applications to make sure I had a place to live after I aged out. Kinda late, right? Well, I had a good reason.

I had a friend who owned a house with a basement to rent for $550 per month. (Pretty cheap for the area.) She wanted to rent it to me, so I was in no hurry to fill out housing applications. (If I hadn't had that basement to rent, I would've filled them out long before!)

Four Months Left

I made up my mind. I would rent the basement apartment and pay my own rent. Why? Because I would be living alone and I like my own space. There's a nice feeling that comes to having my own place. I can do whatever I want to do and no one can say anything about it. Of course, there's a flip side to this. There are bills, bills and more bills, which will be my responsibility alone. But I still want to have my own place.

Now that I decided to have my own apartment, I was really excited to furnish it. I started walking from one end of New York to the other checking out prices on furniture. I wanted a decent bedroom set that would last and a desk where I could study. But, again, I wanted to be careful about money.

I also went to see my apartment and what needed to be done to it for me to live there. That included cleaning up a little, painting and decorating. I'm getting excited about my new life outside of the system... but also nervous.

Three Months to Go!

For the next three months I'm going to concentrate on saving more money. I want to have at least four months of rent put aside to use in case of emergency, and I'm close to reaching that goal. Like I said, I'm nervous but excited. In the meantime, the countdown continues!

Update:

Six months after Giselle wrote this article, she successfully made the transition from living in foster care to living on her own. When she aged out of the system, she had well over $5,000 saved. She also got an internship in community planning which paid her enough to support herself, and which she enjoyed.

Now, five years have passed since Giselle wrote this article. She still lives in the lovely basement apartment—now with her sister and mom—and trains foster youth to speak about their experiences for Voices of Youth.

My Goals for Independence

Read Giselle's story about preparing to leave the system on p. 284.

Now start making your own plan for leaving the system.

This worksheet will help you plan your goals.

GOAL #1:

When I leave the system, my goal is to live _____

_____

_____

_____

If that doesn't work out, my second choice is _____

_____

_____

_____

Some things I will do to help me reach this goal are _____

_____

_____

Challenges to accomplishing this goal are _____

_____

_____

_____

GOAL #2:

When I leave the system, I plan to pay for food and rent by _____

_____

_____

_____

Some things that will help me reach this goal are _____

_____

_____

_____

Challenges to accomplishing this goal are _____

_____

_____

_____

GOAL #3:

When I leave the system, I hope to have saved at least $_____

Take the amount you want to save and divide by the number of weeks until you leave care. (Remember there are 52 weeks in a year.) This is the amount you need to save each week. (For example: $5,000 ÷ 104 weeks = $48 per week.)

Each week I need to save $_____

Some things that will help me reach this goal are _____

_____

_____

_____

Challenges to accomplishing this goal are _____

_____

_____

_____

GOAL #4:

After you leave the system, there will be many times when you need help or support. Use the following chart to list five people who you can count on for support, and specificy how they can help you. For instance, one might be able to drive you to the doctor, another might be able to give you a job recommendation, another might be a good listener if you're going through a rough time.

NAME:	PHONE #	HOW THEY CAN HELP ME

If you weren't able to list five people, make a plan for how to expand your circle of support here.

_____

_____

_____

GOAL #5:

Before I leave the system, I need to learn how to _____

_____

_____

Some things that will help me reach this goal are _____

_____

_____

Challenges to accomplishing this goal are _____

_____

_____

In the Driver's Seat

Setting goals gets you on the road. Here's how to get going.

By XAVIER REYES

How many times have you heard your social worker, teacher or counselor ask you what your goals are? And how many times did you  answer that you didn't know, or just gave them any old answer that would shut them up? As annoying as this question may seem, it's a very important one.

Xavier Reyes

Our goals are important because they help us plan for our future. If we didn't have goals, we would be like drivers without destinations, driving round and round without really going anywhere. Goals help us focus on our dreams and realize the possibilities in our lives.

Goals also let us be in the driver's seat for a change. Too often in foster care we have no say over who we live with, where we live, where we go to school and even what we eat. People are always making plans for us, and we often don't get a say in those plans. Having goals for your future can help you get more control over your life. It can help you be the one determining what's happening to you.

A few years back, when I was living in a group home, one of my goals was to live independently. I set this goal when I was 17 years old, and worked on it until I was 21, the age in New York City when you leave foster care, ready or not.

To achieve my goals I had to make sure that I had two very important things: a roof over my head, and a secure job that was going to pay enough for rent.

Goals and a Game Plan

It took years of work to reach those goals. I had to learn how to find and hold down a job. I had to look for apartments, and convince landlords that I would be a responsible tenant. I was eventually able to get a job as an administrative director in an office (I make lots of phone calls, keep track of paper work, and generally keep things organized.) I found an apartment through my social worker's assistant.

If I hadn't had goals and a game plan for how I was going to reach them, I wouldn't be where I am today. I wouldn't have my own apartment and I sure wouldn't have my job. I might have made it, but I probably would have been working for half of the salary I now make, and would be living in a studio apartment the size of a closet.

So here's another important thing about reaching your goals—it's not just enough to have a goal, you also have to have a game plan, which is a plan for how and when you're going to reach those goals. For instance, to find an apartment before I left care, my game plan was to look in the classified sections for apartments, ask everyone in my agency about apartments, and get together all the things a landlord would want to see—references, paycheck stubs, savings account statements and a social security card.

Putting the Plan Into Action

But having goals and a game plan is just half of it. The other half is actually putting the game plan into action. And if you're like me, this is the hard part—getting off our butts and doing what we need to do to reach our goals.

Before you begin to work on a game plan for reaching your dreams, it's important to know the difference between a strong goal and a weak goal, a realistic goal and an unrealistic goal.

> **Too often in foster care we have no say over who we live with, where we live, where we go to school and even what we eat.**

Weak goals are goals that you are going to achieve whether or not you really put work into it. For example, setting a goal to make money is a weak goal. Why? 'Cause one way or another you will make money one day. This goal is too broad. So how can you change this weak goal into a strong goal? Instead of saying, "My goal is to make money," you can say, "My goal is to make $25,000 a year by the time I am 25 years old."

The more specific you are in your goal, the clearer it will be, and the more likely it is that you will get exactly what you want. Not half of it.

An unrealistic goal is to say that you want to be a doctor by the time you are 23, knowing that you are 17 and haven't even taken Advanced Placement science classes in high school. A realistic goal is to say that you want to be in nursing school (or whatever you want) by the time you are 23. This is realistic because you are giving yourself enough time to get the education and experience you need to reach your goal. You can always go to medical school later if that's still your goal.

> **A good, strong goal is one that is measurable, clear and achievable. The more specific and focused your goal is, the better chance you will have of reaching it.**

Finding Your Goals

A good, strong goal is one that is measurable (you know you achieved it if you are making $25,000 when you are 25), that is very clear, and that is achievable. The more specific and focused your goal is, the better chance you will have at reaching it.

A good way to focus your goals and start a game plan is to:

1. Write a list of goals that you want to accomplish for yourself, both in the short-term and in the long-term. Look at each goal and decide which goals are realistic and which goals are unrealistic. (For example, it's unlikely you'll become a rap star or pro athlete.)

2. Now take the same list and remove the goals that you know are going to happen regardless of anything. (Remove "Leave foster care by age 21." That will happen no matter what.) Once you narrow it down, list your goals in the order of importance. (Getting that new outfit is not more important than getting that job you need!)

3. Now that you have a good list of goals, write each goal on a separate piece of paper. For each goal, write out three or four actions that you know you must take in order to reach that goal. For example, let's say my goal is to get a job, then my steps might be: 1) Get typing speed up to 40 words per minute 2) Learn Microsoft Word 3) Write a resume 4) Look for a job.

You probably want to break the steps down more. For instance, to look for a job, I might write: a) Go directly to at least 10 places I want to be hired and ask about job openings b) See the job counselor at my school about job openings c) Ask my social worker if she knows of job openings d) Apply at temp agencies.

4. After you come up with actions for each goal, write a date when you are going to complete the step.

5. Stick to the plan. The hardest part in achieving your goals is not setting the goal, but seeing it through. Stick with the plan and complete the steps you need to achieve your goal. Don't let yourself keep putting it off.

In the words of Derek Canty, a workshop facilitator with the Grassroots Aspen Experience, where I also lead workshops, "Life don't care if you are sick or tired. Life goes on with or without you."

It's up to you to take the necessary steps to achieve your goals. No one is going to give you a break or a free handout. If you want something, get up and make it happen for yourself. You can do it.

My Plan for Independence

☐ *Read Xavier's steps to accomplishing goals on page 294.*

☐ *Pick one goal you want to accomplish before leaving foster care. (For help doing this, see page 289.)*

☐ *To make a plan for accomplishing your goal, fill out the chart on the next page (see the example below).*

EXAMPLE:

One goal I want to accomplish before leaving foster care is to:

get a job.

Three steps I will need to take to accomplish that goal are:

1. Get typing speed up to 40 words per minute

2. Learn Microsoft Word (basics)

3. Write a resume

to be completed by:

the end of month

to be completed by:

two weeks from today

to be completed by:

next week

GOAL #1:

One goal I want to accomplish before leaving foster care is to:

_____

_____

Three steps I will need to take to accomplish that goal are:

1. _____   2. _____   3. _____

_____   _____   _____

_____   _____   _____

_____   _____   _____

_____   _____   _____

to be completed by: to be completed by: to be completed by:

_____   _____   _____

_____   _____   _____

GOAL #2:

One goal I want to accomplish before leaving foster care is to:

_____

_____

Three steps I will need to take to accomplish that goal are:

1. _____   2. _____   3. _____

_____   _____   _____

_____   _____   _____

_____   _____   _____

to be completed by: to be completed by: to be completed by:

_____   _____   _____

_____   _____   _____

GOAL #3:

One goal I want to accomplish before leaving foster care is to:

_____

_____

Three steps I will need to take to accomplish that goal are:

1. _____   2. _____   3. _____

_____   _____   _____

_____   _____   _____

_____   _____   _____

_____   _____   _____

to be completed by: to be completed by: to be completed by:

_____   _____   _____

_____   _____   _____

To All Foster Youth:

You can overcome the madness

By MARIO DRUMMONDS

Mario Drummonds knows a lot about overcoming obstacles and achieving success. Mario, who spent 17 years in foster care, is now head

Mario Drummonds

of the Northern Manhattan Perinatal Partnership, an agency in New York that provides health care and support services for children and parents. He gave this speech to foster youth attending an independent living conference in New York in April 1998:

Many years ago I was awakened by strange voices in my mother's apartment in Harlem.

They were workers from the child welfare agency. My mother was in the next room with a strange man, using heroin.

I remember being placed in a tub with one of my sisters to get washed up in preparation for our first foster home placement.

I always knew something was wrong, but I just followed the case workers with two of my sisters on the way to our first foster home in St. Albans, Queens.

This was the beginning of my journey of 17 years through the foster care system of New York City.

All of you know the real deal:

■ Thinking all the time of going home to Mommy, but somehow not getting there.

■ Unexplained moves from one home to the next.

■ Missing friends you made in the neighborhood, school and parks.

■ Being treated as a second-hand person and wanting to have real parents.

■ Hating being called a foster kid.

■ Watching your sister or brother cry when it's time to move to the next home, because the foster parent did not want to care any longer.

- Wishing you had a new, warm winter coat like the young lady you lived with, who happened to be the real daughter of the foster parent.

- Sitting up in your room with your sisters until 3 p.m. on Christmas Day, hearing the foster family open their gifts and share Christmas Day.

- Doubting yourself and not having faith that you can achieve.

- Believing that you were less than the other kids in the neighborhood.

During my stay in care, I experienced all of these things.

But my message to you is that despite all of these negative situations, you can overcome the madness and achieve your goal of independence.

The program that worked for me I call: "Becoming Greater Than Yourself."

This is a process of self-reflection, development and renewing your human spirit to achieve.

1. Create a Vision of Yourself Beyond Your Current Circumstances

Yes, today all of your are in foster care, but to get out of this situation you must imagine another status for yourself.

When I was a kid, I imagined in my small room that I would play football, own my own company, go to college, and become a social worker despite everyone telling me I would not amount to anything.

Define your own future. If you can't visualize success or something greater than your present self, you will never achieve independence.

So you want to be a D.J.? Be it! Own your own beauty shop? Think it, do it! A lawyer? A social worker? Dream it! Do it!

2. You Must Transcend Fear!

Everybody is fearful of something. However, the folks that succeed accept that they are afraid, then transcend that fear and get the job done to move toward their goals.

I was...

- Afraid to attend Columbia University

www.youthcomm.org

- Afraid to start my own business

- Afraid of building and sustaining intimate relationships

But you must gain your composure, focus on your goals, and turn fear into a technique that will help prepare you for success.

3. Be Willing To Work Harder Than the Average Person

To become greater than yourself, you must be willing to outwork the competition.

Many folks don't believe that you can succeed anyway.

I never had an independent living program when I was in care, but you need to go to those workshops. You must focus on your goals and complete the work to get there. You can't always depend on going home to your mother or father. Adoption may not be an option. In the end, all that you have is your soul, yourself and your close loved ones.

> **Define your own future. If you can't visualize success or something greater than your present self, you will never achieve independence.**

Once you understand your power, you will be able to transcend the welfare line and start your own business or land a decent job.

Once you understand your power, the police vamping down on you won't matter because you will know your rights and stand up to injustice.

Once you understand where you have come from, you will not want your children to enter foster care. Brothers will become caring fathers to their children, and some sisters will stop placing their dead babies behind a toilet bowl.

4. Finally, To Become Greater Than Yourself, You Must Be Willing To Embrace Change

You must be willing to forgive your parents for creating the conditions that made you end up in foster care in the first place.

You must take that chip off of your shoulder, blaming everyone else for your situation, and do something about changing it.

You must be willing to take responsibility for your own life—by getting your own apartment, job and forming your own healthy relationships.

You must be willing to admit that you do have some weakness, and begin the long, tired work of turning your weaknesses into strength.

I call this "shedding skin." This can be a very painful experience. Sometimes folks get afraid and return to the old ways of thinking, acting and believing. However, I believe that all of you out there can take this personal journey. The staff at your agencies, your parents and your friends are there for you if you fall. However, you must lead.

You must become greater than yourself.

Take care of yourselves, brothers and sisters. I feel you, I respect you, I support you and I love you. Thank you for making me whole again, by allowing me to tell my story. I have become greater than myself and it is all that!

Peace.

www.youthcomm.org

This Is to Certify That

_____

(name)

On This Day of

_____

(date)

Having Studied This Book and Completed the Following Worksheets:

☐ My Budget (p. 54)
☐ My Job Interview (p. 84)
☐ My First Apartment (p. 112)
☐ My Support System (p. 147)
☐ My Self-Care Plan (p. 163)
☐ My Recipes (p. 181)
☐ My Goals for Independence (p. 289)
☐ My Plan for Independence (p. 298)

Is Officially Ready to Embark on the Journey of Life After Foster Care.

Congratulations!

Acknowledgments

This book is made possible by the courage, talent and hard work of young people in foster care who wrote about their experiences. They are part of a much larger group of young people at *Represent* who have written about their lives since 1993. We are moved and inspired by all of them.

Many foundations, corporations, and individuals support Youth Communciation's work to train teens in foster care to tell their stories. We would like to thank the Altman Foundation, Andrus Foundation, Annenberg Foundation, Annie E. Casey Foundation, Child Welfare Fund, Cricket Island Foundation, Henry van Ameringen, Ira DeCamp Foundation, Jim Casey Initiative, Kenworthy-Swift Foundation, Morgan Stanley Foundation, New York City Department of Youth and Community Development, New York Community Trust, The New York Times Company Foundation, Open Society Institute, Pinkerton Foundation, Public Welfare Foundation, Rita & Stanley Kaplan Foundation, Spunk Fund, Inc., W. Clement and Jessie B. Stone Foundation, Surdna Foundation, Tides Foundation, Time Warner, W.T. Grant Foundation, and the many individuals who have contributed to our work.

About Youth Communication

Youth Communication is a nonprofit youth development program located in New York City whose mission is to teach writing, journalism, and leadership skills. The teenagers we train, most of whom are New York City public high school students, become writers for our two teen-written publications, *New Youth Connections*, a general-interest youth magazine, and *Foster Care Youth United* (now known as *Represent*), a magazine by and for young people in foster care.

Youth Communication was founded in 1980 by Keith Hefner in response to a nationwide study which found that censorship, mediocrity, and racial exclusion had crippled the high school press. Hefner is the recipient of a Charles H. Revson Fellowship on the future of the City of New York from Columbia University and the Luther P. Jackson Excellence in Education Award of the New York Association of Black Journalists. In 1989 he won a MacArthur Fellowship for his work at Youth Communication.

Each year, more than one hundred young people participate in Youth Communication's school-year and summer journalism workshops, where they work under the direction of several full-time adult editors. They come from every corner of New York City, and most are African American, Latino, or Asian. Many are recent immigrants. For these writers, the opportunity to reach their peers with accurate portrayals of their lives and important self-help information motivates them to create powerful stories.

Teachers, counselors, social workers, and other adults circulate our magazines to young people in their classes and after-school youth programs. They distribute 70,000 copies of *New Youth Connections* each month during the school year, and 10,000 bi-monthly copies of *Represent*. Teachers and counselors tell us that the teens they work with—including many who are ordinarily resistant to reading—clamor for these publications. Teen readers report that the information and inspiration in our stories help them reflect on their lives and open lines of communication with parents and teachers.

www.youthcomm.org

Running a strong youth development program while simultaneously producing quality teen magazines requires us to be sensitive to the complicated lives and emotions of the teen participants while also providing an intellectually rigorous experience. We achieve that goal in the writing/teaching/editing relationship, which is the core of our program.

Our teaching and editorial process begins with discussions between adult editors and the teen staff, during which they seek to discover the stories that are most important to each teen writer and that will also appeal to a significant segment of our readers.

Once topics have been chosen, students begin the process of crafting their stories. For a personal story, that means revisiting events in one's past to understand their significance for the future. For a commentary, it means developing a logical and persuasive point of view. For a reported story, it means gathering information through research and interviews. Students look inward and outward as they try to make sense of their experiences and the world around them and find the points of intersection between personal and social concerns. That process can take a few weeks or a few months. Stories frequently go through four, five, or more drafts as students work under the guidance of their editors, the way any professional writer does.

Many of the students who walk through our doors have uneven skills, as a result of poor education, living under extremely stressful conditions, or coming from homes where English is a second language. Yet, to complete their stories, students must successfully perform a wide range of activities, including writing and rewriting, reading, discussion, reflection, research, interviewing, and typing. They must work as members of a team and they must accept a great deal of individual responsibility. They learn to verify facts and cope with rejection. They engage in explorations of truthfulness and fairness. They meet deadlines. They must develop the audacity to believe that they have something important to say and the humility to recognize that saying it well is not a process of instant gratification, but usually requires a long, hard struggle through many discussions and much rewriting.

It would be impossible to teach these skills and dispositions as separate, disconnected topics, like grammar, ethics, or assertiveness. However, we find that students make rapid progress when they are learning skills in the context of an inquiry that is personally significant to them and that they think will benefit their peers.

Writers usually participate in our program for one semester, though some stay much longer. Years later, many of them report that working here was a turning point in their lives—that it helped them acquire the confidence and skills that they needed for success in their subsequent education and careers. Scores of our graduates have overcome tremendous obstacles to become journalists, writers, and novelists. Hundreds more are working in law, teaching, business, and other careers. Many former Youth Communication teen staffers have made careers of writing, including National Book Award finalist Edwidge Danticat (*Krik? Krak!*), novelist James Earl Hardy (*B-Boy Blues*), writer Veronica Chambers (*Mama's Girl*), and *New York Times* reporter Rachel Swarns.

For information about our publications and programs see www.youthcomm.org. Contributions to Youth Communication are tax deductible to the fullest extent of the law.

Web Resources

Magazines by Teens in Care

Represent: The Voice of Youth in Care, www.youthcomm.org
National magazine written by and for teens in care.
Mockingbird Times, www.mockingbirdsociety.org
Washington State magazine written by and for teens in care.

Books & Films

Aging Out, www.pbs.org/wnet/agingout/index-hi.html
PBS film with powerful profiles of three teens as they age out of care.
On Their Own, by Martha Shirk and Gary Stangler
Profiles of 10 teens who have aged out of the foster care system.
Youth Advocacy Center, www.youthadvocacycenter.org
Publisher of *Beyond the Foster Care System: The Future for Teens*,
a book and training program for independent living.
Youth Communication, www.youthcomm.org
Youth Communication publishes dozens of books (in addition to this one) about the
foster care experience.

Help for Teens and Young Adults

California Youth Connection, www.calyouthconn.org
California statewide membership and advocacy organization for youth in care.
FosterClub.com
Website with many resources and activities for teens in care.
Orphan Foundation of America, www.orphan.org
Information on scholarships, mentoring, and more.
Foster Care Alumni of America, www.fostercarealumni.org
Organization of foster care alumni for advocacy and connection.

Resources for Adults Who Work With Teens

Child Welfare League of America, www.cwla.org
National organization of foster care providers.
Daniel Memorial, Inc., www.danielkids.org
Training and materials for independent living. Conferences. Catalog.
Independent Living Resources, Inc., www.ilrinc.com
Training and materials for independent living. Conferences. Catalog.
Jim Casey Youth Opportunities Initiative, www.jimcaseyyouth.org
Runs projects in several major cities to help teens in care transition to adulthood.
National Foster Care Coalition, www.nationalfostercare.org
Information and advocacy for government support of foster care.
National Independent Living Association, www.nilausa.org
Membership organization for independent living programs and staff.
National Resource Center for Foster Care and Permanency Planning,
www.hunter.cuny.edu/socwork/nrcfcpp/
Training, technical assistance, and information for child welfare agencies.
National Resource Center for Youth Services, www.nrcys.ou.edu
Training and materials for independent living. Conferences. Catalog.
Social Learning, www.sociallearning.com
Materials for independent living. Catalog.

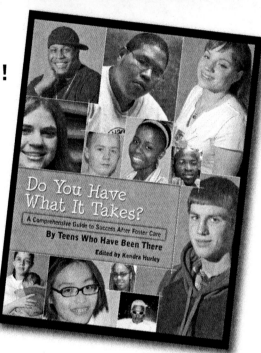